Indians of the Northern Plains

by William K. Powers

An American Indians Then & Now Book

Earl Schenck Miers, General Editor

Capricorn Books, New York

TO CHARLES T. CRANE

CAPRICORN BOOKS EDITION 1973
Copyright © 1969 by William K. Powers
All rights reserved. Published simultaneously in Canada
by Longman Canada Limited, Toronto.
SBN 399-50277-7
Library of Congress Catalog Card Number: 69-11855
PRINTED IN THE UNITED STATES OF AMERICA

Contents

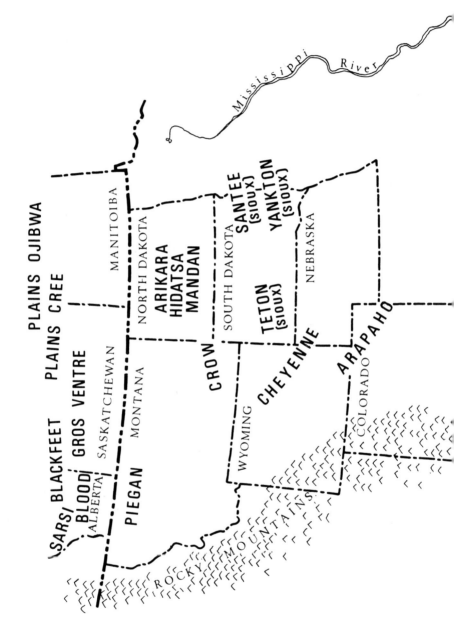

Introduction

The Northern Plains Indian enjoys a worldwide reputation of being the "typical" Indian of Hollywood and television fame. Not only has he impressed non-Indians with his magnificent eagle feather warbonnet, his ability to ride bareback at breakneck speed, his unquenchable thirst for enemy scalps, and his universal sign language; he has succeeded in modern historic times even in influencing Indians from other parts of the country. Today, among most tribes, to be Indian is synonymous with being a Plains Indian.

But it was not always so. Anthropologists have divided the North American continent into various culture areas, geographic regions in which tribes behaved in the same manner, used the same kinds of animals for food, clothing, and shelter, and had the same attitudes about hunting, warfare, and domestic life. The Great Plains is one such area, or, more correctly, two areas—the Northern High Plains and the Southern Plains and Prairie. In this book we will meet the Indians of the Northern Plains.

Although the Plains Indians may have seemed similar as a group in the eyes of Europeans and non-Plains Indians, there were a great number of characteristics which differed from tribe to tribe. Language, for instance, was different, as were political structure, religious belief, and material culture. Some Northern Plains tribes lived in the well-known tipi, while others lived in earth lodges. Some tribes were peaceful, some warlike; others formed loose confederacies to prevent their annihilation by hostile tribes.

Since hunting was the primary source of food on the Plains, larger tribes were often divided into bands and even subbands for the purpose of finding enough game to fill their individual needs. Even the tribes that lived in permanent villages and farmed left their homes in the winter to follow the game.

In this book we will investigate those Indian tribes which, before the white man came, ruled a vast empire on the North American continent. Today, these tribes, now removed to reservations, are often referred to as the vanishing race, but current census reports indicate that the Indian population is growing in such proportion that soon there will be more Indians in the United States than there were when Columbus arrived. Not only is the American Indian rapidly multiplying; he is beginning to rejuvenate fervent interest in the ways of his forefathers. We are, in fact, today witnessing an Indian renaissance that will eventually lead the Indian to his rightful place in the history of the United States —a place too often denied the first Americans.

1 Before the White Man

THE GREAT PLAINS is a gigantic swath of land bordered on the north by the Canadian Plains of Saskatchewan and parts of Alberta and Manitoba, on the south by the Gulf of Mexico, on the east by the Mississippi River, and on the west by the Rocky Mountains. It comprises 1,500,000 square miles of land, an area approximately one-third the land surface of the United States.

The state of South Dakota, the geographic center of the Great Plains, is known as the Land of Infinite Variety. This name applies well to the Great Plains itself, for there is no single characteristic that best describes the climate and terrain. The land is generally arid, with an average rainfall of 20 inches. In summer the temperature soars to more than 100 degrees, while in some parts it drops to 40 below in the long winter months. The altitude ranges from sea level to more than 13,000 feet in the highlands of Wyoming and Montana.

Starting from Texas and heading northward, one notices the great expanses of flatland in Kansas and southern Nebraska, the beautiful rolling hills and pine-dotted buttes of northern Nebraska and South Dakota, which in the northern part of the latter state break into the famous Badlands and Black Hills. To the west lie the sage-lined hills of Wyoming and farther west, the great Big Horn Mountains. There is more terrain like the Badlands in North Dakota and, again, more flatlands, which level off, continuing into Saskatchewan. The gently rolling hills of Montana break miraculously into high mountains in the western part of the state.

In it is the northwestern part of the Great Plains that we find the original homes of the Indians discussed in this book: the Assiniboine; the Blackfeet Federation, including the Northern Blackfeet, Piegan, and Blood; the Teton, Yankton, and Santee divisions of the great Sioux Nation; the Sarsi, Crow, Gros Ventre, Cheyenne, and Arapaho; the Arikara, Mandan, and Hidatsa; and the Plains Cree and Plains Ojibwa.

To understand just where the Indians of the Northern Plains lived in historic times look at the map on page 6. There is archeological evidence that the ancestors of the Great Plains tribes lived on the North American continent 10,000 to 11,000 years ago, but the Plains Indian with which we deal is relatively recent to the area. There is also historic evidence that certain of the Northern Plains tribes lived there before the others migrated to the Plains from other areas. The Blackfeet, Arapaho, Gros Ventre, Mandan, Hidatsa, and Arikara, for instance lived there before the other tribes came to the Northern Plains from their original homelands in the East and Northeast. For the most part, these latter tribes were driven from their original homes by their warlike neighbors, who had received guns from the French and English traders; others sought to follow the trail of the buffalo herds onto the Plains.

At the time Columbus arrived, there were an estimated 1,000,000 Indians living in North America. According to population estimates made for 1780, the Great Plains—including the Northern and Southern Plains and Prairie—was the home of approximately 150,000 Indians representing 28 principal tribes and numerous subtribes and bands. Some of these tribes, such as the Sioux and Blackfeet, formed confederacies, thus making them powerful warrior nations. At times, these confederacies weakened, the members fighting among themselves; while, at other times, smaller tribes, such as the Sarsi, were forced to join a larger tribe (the Blackfeet) for their own protection against marauders.

While the Indians of the Upper Missouri—the Mandan, Hidatsa, and Arikara—were horticultural tribes, raising corn, beans, squash, and pumpkins in their fortified village gardens, most of the Plains tribes were nomads, constantly in search of game and warfare with other tribes. These peripatetic bands lived in conical skin tents, called tipis, from the Sioux word for dwelling.

Their very lives depended on the buffalo, which is estimated to have numbered 60,000,000 before the white man came. At one time this great beast could be found in all parts of the North American continent, but by the time of the white man's arrival, most of the herds had migrated to the Western Plains. Early reports say there were so many buffalo "you could walk across the Plains on their backs."

To the Indian the buffalo was the source of all life.

Even the horticultural tribes left their villages in the wintertime to hunt them or traded their produce for buffalo meat and hides in the summer.

A major part of the lives of the nomadic tribes was spent in hunting buffalo. Before the horse appeared on the Plains, buffalo were hunted on foot, sometimes being stampeded over great precipices, where they fell to their deaths. After the introduction of the horse, the buffalo were chased on horseback, a dangerous technique adding adventure to the spirit of the hunt. Usually the men did the hunting while the women followed behind to skin the animals and butcher the carcasses. Boys learned to hunt by chasing buffalo calves.

Legends state that the buffalo was put on the earth by the Great Spirit solely for the use of Indian people, and the whole world of the Plains Indian revolved around its many uses. Many of the Indians considered it a representative of the deities and performed sacred buffalo dances to insure good hunting. Sacred persons were said to have the ability to sing certain songs which would entice the buffalo to come near their camps, while others were allegedly endowed with the ability to cure the sick by using special buffalo medicines and praying to the spirit of the buffalo. One of the most sacred objects found in camp was the buffalo skull, which was used in many ceremonies.

Illimitable uses were made of the creature. From its shaggy hide, came the skins required to make tipis and moccasins, robes, and other clothing. Buffalo provided the prize meat; buffalo tongue was a delicacy, as were the heart and kidneys, which were sometimes eaten on the spot where the animal was slain. Women made all their daily cooking and sewing utensils from the sinew and bones of the animal. Children made toys from its bones. One authority estimates that there were more than 300 uses for the buffalo. The buffalo, no doubt, was the single most important means of sustenance for the Plains dwellers, and it was only after its wanton destruction by ruthless white sportsmen that the spirit of the Indian was crushed.

There was a time when the Plains Indian traveled and hunted on foot whenever he sought buffalo or new camping grounds. Even war journeys were made on foot. During this time the tipis were smaller and were dragged from place to place by dogs. Dogs were used to carry most of the small camp items, either in packs strapped to their backs or on a V-shaped drag called a travois.

Then came the event that gave dramatic change to the life of the Plains Indian. In the eighteenth century the horse made its first appearance.

It has been resolved that the horse originally came to the Northern Plains from the Spanish in the Southwest and was traded from one tribe to another. It is possible that the Spanish taught some of their Indian slaves how to ride and care for horses. It is through these horse-trained Indians that the horse began to be dispersed northward over the Southern Plains, finally reaching the Northern Plains during the period 1720–1784.

Horses quickly revolutionized the culture and economy of the Plains Indians. Now entire camps could be moved quickly and easily; tipis could be made larger, with the dog travois now adapted to the horse. Tribes could also strike deathly blows at their enemies and retreat before revenge was taken. But most of all, the buffalo could now be chased at his own speed by mounted hunters who discharged their arrows riding at breakneck speed.

Because of the usefulness of the horse, it became a status symbol, an indication of wealth, and a highly prized trade item. Tribes raided one another for the sole purpose of capturing coveted horse herds. To own many horses was a sign of influence and prestige, and to give horses away to the needy was a prime virtue.

Although most of the Plains Indians increased their nomadism with the introduction of the horse, the Upper Missouri tribes remained semisedentary horticulturists. They were also among the best known of horse traders. Even before the white man's arrival, trade had existed among some of the friendly Indian tribes. The Arikara, for instance, went as far as the foot of the Black Hills to trade with the Kiowa, Kiowa-Apache, Comanche (who later moved to the Southern Plains), and the Cheyenne and Arapaho. The Crow also traded with the Mandan and Hidatsa, and one of the best known trade fairs was conducted by the Sioux on the Saint James River in the present state of South Dakota.

The Indians of the Northern Plains soon became the finest horsemen in the world. The famous Indian fighter General Philip Sheridan called them "the greatest light cavalry in the world." The horse influenced virtually every aspect of Plains culture, including the tribal language, to which were added hundreds of new words associated with riding, maintaining, and outfitting it. Ceremonies were developed to honor the horse, and many involved the retelling of stories about the coming of this strange beast.

Although the Indians of the Northern Plains fought one another over hunting grounds and sought vengeance against one another over the loss of warriors in battle, they were all related culturally. One of the most significant of the cultural traits was the participation of each tribe in an annual religious celebration known as the Sun dance.

To many tribes the sun was the symbol, the manifestation, of the Great Spirit. In the Sun dance the Indian offered himself up to his god, sometimes inflicting himself with torture as the ultimate sacrifice. Many Sun dancers, however, simply danced for a prescribed number of days gazing full into the sun; hence its name.

While the Sun dance varied in ritual from one tribe to the next, it was generally danced once a year by warriors who had made a vow while on the warpath. If a warrior and his group were faced with annihilation, for example, he might cry out that if his party reached safety, he would offer himself up at the next Sun dance. The vow was made aloud so that all his warriors heard him, and it was impossible to revoke the pledge once it was spoken.

Despite the seriousness of the Sun dance, it was also a time for entertainment and visiting with friends. It was an occasion—sometimes the only occasion during the year's time—when all the scattered bands of a nomadic tribe could converge. And so there was much frivolity and merrymaking in the evening, when the sun had set and the dancers had retired to await the first few streaks of sunlight the next morning.

Religion, aside from the Sun dance, played an important part in the lives of the Indian people. Part of becoming a man demanded that a youth at puberty seek out the advice of an older man, usually a shaman, or medicine man, for the purpose of going on a vision quest. The young man would be told to go to a hill outside the village, where he would fast and pray until he received a vision. In this vision the spirits would give him certain instructions and possibly a good luck charm to protect against evil or make him a strong hunter or warrior. When he returned to the village, he would meet again with the old man, who would interpret his vision. The boy would be instructed to go out and kill a certain kind of bird or animal, whose skin, or some other part, would be used as the youngster's good luck charm.

Men, too, went on the vision quest whenever they sought supernatural aid. They would leave the camp and climb a lonely hill, where they fasted and prayed, awaiting the vision. In their visions, they might be instructed in new songs and dances or methods by which they could insure success in hunting and warfare. Shamans and medicine men often sought to renew their mystical powers to cure the sick by going on vision quests, for it was believed that the more a man sought visions, the more powerful he became. Upon returning to the camp, it was sometimes necessary for the man to reenact his vision for all the people in camp.

Another important element in the religious life of the Plains Indian was the sweat lodge ceremony. Often before going on a vision quest or participating in one of the important ceremonies, such as the Sun dance, the men took a sweat bath. In addition to its salutary benefits, the Indians believed the sweat lodge to be a special place in which they could pray. Among some tribes the men would emerge from the sweat bath and plunge into an icy stream or river—whether in summer or winter. The Sweat Lodge was considered a renewal of life, and each man left the ceremony with a feeling of well-being, both spiritual and physical.

The Indian lived in a world of supernatural happenings. He lived close to nature and believed that spirits inhabited every object, animate and inaminate. Thus, an Indian might pray to a rock, the wind, the four directions, the sun and moon, or the buffalo, all of which were the personifications of the Great Spirit or of lesser spirits who controlled the people and animals. The Indian believed in a hereafter, a place where game was plentiful and people lived at peace with the Old Ones. Here he would also enjoy the adventures of warfare against the spirits of his worldly enemies. He believed, too, that the ghosts of the departed freely roamed the earth and that they were something that the common person must avoid, or he would cross the shadow of a ghost and be killed. Certain men, however, could communicate with the ghosts and were considered sacred. There was a great belief in witchcraft, sorcery, and prediction of the future.

The Indian believed that he could pray to a benevolent god to seek the power to do good and to a malevolent god for the power to do evil. It is unlikely that the old-time Indians ever prayed to one god, although there were some chief gods among the ranks of deities. Most tribes prayed with the long-stemmed pipe, believing that the smoke of the pipe carried their prayers upward. The eagle was considered a messenger of the Great Spirit and thus was revered.

There were also cults among the Northern Plains

Indians made up of men who had dreamed of lightning. In so doing, they were bound to act in an antinatural manner for the rest of their lives. In the summer they would wear heavy clothing and run around sparsely clad in the winter. They would stick their hands in boiling water, claiming that it was ice cold or on a hot day complain it was freezing. For the rest of their lives they did everything contrarily. The people often called them "clowns." However, their actions were a result of deep convictions about the power of lightning. If they did not act foolishly, they believed that they might be struck by lightning. Certain women who were known as herbalists were also fearful of lightning and believed that if they did not observe certain customs or say certain prayers before digging for herbs, they, too, would be struck.

The dead were buried on scaffolds, in trees, or in lone tipis. In each case the favorite belongings of the deceased were placed with the body. For a man, his favorite horse was killed so that he might ride the spirit of the horse into the next life. He was dressed in his finest clothing, and sufficient food was placed alongside his body. A woman was also buried in her favorite clothes, and her special cooking and sewing utensils were placed beside her.

One of the most colorful groups of the Northern Plains Indians was the soldier, or warrior societies, which were composed of men upon whom fell the responsibility of maintaining order. They were empowered to deal with anyone who broke the rules of the camp or hunt. In the buffalo hunt, for instance, a sudden charge by one man might frighten away the herd before the rest of the hunters could ride in for the kill. If someone disobeyed the commands of the soldiers, he might be punished severely, his tipi cut to pieces, weapons broken, and horses shot. Sometimes the offender was killed.

There were also other societies, sometimes organized by ages, which were primarily war associations, and the members went on war journeys as a group. Other associations were formed for purely social activities. Women had their own societies, often resembling a women's quilting club. They got together to tan robes or make clothing and tipis. Some were comprised of women who were the relatives of warriors.

2 The People

IN DESCRIBING groups of Indians, we usually refer to tribes, nations, and confederacies, the meanings of which are not always clear. It can be said that a tribe shared the same language, religious beliefs, methods of decorating clothing and paraphernalia, and pledged allegiance to other members of the same tribe before members of neighboring tribes. "Nation" and "confederacy" are often used interchangeably to indicate an alliance of tribes—for example, the Northern Blackfeet, Piegan, and Blood tribes, along with the Gros Ventre (Atsina) and Sarsi, formed the Blackfeet Confederacy. The three main divisions of the Sioux—the Teton, Yankton, and Santee—formed what is often called the Sioux Nation. The tribes belonging to such a confederacy did not necessarily speak the same language, as is the case of the Blackfeet. Or sometimes, as is exemplified by the Sioux, the member tribes spoke dialects of the same language, similar enough to be mutually intelligible by all.

Tribes were often divided into bands or clans. These were smaller political units, which were formed because the land could not provide for large groups of people. During the summer months these bands usually divided and went their own ways to hunt. Irregularly they banded together to go on war journeys and at least once a year for the Sun dance. Memberships in a band had no rigid requirements; families could leave one band and join another at will. Clans, however, were determined by kinship.

Nationalism was, and still is to a great extent, unknown among the Northern Plains Indian. Therefore, a Crow considered himself primarily a member of the Crow tribe before he considered himself an "Indian."

In addition to tribal traits, each tribe shared a somewhat different history. Some were friendly with the white man, some bitter enemies. In this chapter we will meet each of the principal tribes of the Northern Plains and learn about some of the historic and cultural traits that made each tribe distinctive.

The Arapaho

The Arapaho, Algonkian speakers who lived in Nebraska, Kansas, and parts of Colorado and Wyoming, originally migrated onto the Plains from the east, where they had lived in earth-covered lodges on the western shore of Lake Superior. The name Arapaho comes from the Pawnee word *tirapihu,* meaning "he buys, or trades" and indicating one of the prime activities of this tribe. They called themselves Inuna-ina, meaning, our people, a common designation for many of the Northern Plains tribes. The Sioux and other Plains tribes called them the Blue Cloud people, but the exact interpretation of this has been lost. In 1780 the population of the Arapaho was estimated at 3,000.

A group of Arapaho Indians at the Omaha Exposition, 1898, photographed by F. A. Rinehart of the Bureau of American Ethnology.

The Arapaho have been historically linked with the Cheyenne, who also sometimes united with the Kiowa and Comanche of the Southern Plains to raid against the Mexican settlements in the Southwest. They most often battled against the Shoshoni, Ute, Navajo, and Pawnee, and some Arapaho were with the Sioux when the latter tribe annihilated George Armstrong Custer and the Seventh Cavalry at the Battle of the Little Big Horn, June 25, 1876.

The Arapaho are considered one of the most religious people on the Northern Plains. In their present-day ceremonies they make use of a tubular ceremonial pipe, unlike the elbow- or T-shaped pipes popular on the Plains. They still have their annual Sun dance, which is conducted in a circular medicine lodge on the Wind River Reservation in Wyoming. This impressive ceremony draws many other tribes.

The Arapaho made a treaty with the United States in 1861 at Fort Wise, Kansas, and signed the Medicine Lodge treaty in 1867. They were divided into the Northern and Southern Arapaho, the northern group being placed on a reservation at Wind River, which they share with their traditional enemies of old, the Shoshoni. The Southern Arapaho were removed to Oklahoma, where they live with their traditional allies, the Cheyenne. The northern group, along with the Shoshoni, presently number 4,400, and the southern group, together with the Cheyenne, number approximately 3,000.

Many of the Arapaho are still friendly with the Sioux and today make frequent trips to the Pine Ridge Reservation, where they participate in the Sweat Lodge and other religious ceremonies with their Sioux neighbors. Some of the Arapaho have also intermarried with the Sioux.

The Arikara

The name Arikara (sometimes spelled Aricaree or shortened to Ree) refers to a headdress worn by members of the tribe, in which two bones resembling horns were placed upright on the head.

The Arikara, with their neighbors, the Mandan and Hidatsa, formed a unique culture on the Northern Plains. Unlike their nomadic enemies, the Sioux and

Assiniboine, the Arikara lived in fortified villages along the Missouri River in the present state of North Dakota. Along with the Mandan and Hidatsa, they are often referred to as the Upper Missouri River tribes.

The Arikara migrated onto the Plains along with the Pawnee and Wichita of the Southern Plains, with which they speak a similar Caddoan language. It is said that the Caddoan speakers originally came from the Southeast and migrated northward from the Southern Plains. In 1780 the Arikara population was estimated at 3,800.

The Arikara lived in the midst of a highly developed culture. Their villages were fortified by stockade fences and trenches, which prevented any attack from raiding tribes. They were divided into twelve villages, which were represented by four men in councils, each man being elected to represent three of his tribes.

They were horticulturists and raised corn, beans, squash, pumpkins, and tobacco, which they traded with other tribes. During the winter months they left their villages to hunt for buffalo. They made a fine grade of pottery and baskets, another indication of their highly developed culture.

The Arikara were exceptional horse traders, and it is from this tribe that many of the tribes who originally lived in the Great Lakes regions obtained their horses. It is estimated that they themselves received their first horses from the Kiowa and Comanche in about the latter part of the 1730's. Prior to this time, they, like other Plains tribes, used dogs to transport their belongings. Early travelers among the Arikara note the unusually large numbers of dogs—sometimes thirty to forty— which were owned by each Arikara family.

Portraits of two Assiniboine men painted by Carl Bodmer, June 29, 1833, at Fort Union.

Today the Arikara share the Fort Berthold Reservation in North Dakota with their old friends the Mandan and Hidatsa, where they are collectively known as the Three Affiliated Tribes. The reservation is composed of nearly 250,000 acres, and the combined tribes have a population of 2,250.

The Assiniboine

It is estimated that at one time the Assiniboine were the largest tribe on the Northern Plains, numbering a possible 28,000 strong. They controlled that territory now known as Minnesota, North Dakota, and parts of Montana, Manitoba, Saskatchewan, and Alberta.

The name Assiniboine is a corruption of a Ojibwa Indians' word meaning stone boilers and alluding to their method of cooking meat by placing hot stones in a pouch of water to make the water boil. They were Siouan speakers and called themselves Nakota, meaning allied, or affiliated. They were originally a part of the Yankton Sioux but later broke away from their parent tribe. In Canada they are referred to as the Stoney, or Stonies, again referring to their method of boiling water.

The Assiniboine were originally estimated at being comprised of thirty-three bands which roamed the Plains freely, seeking buffalo and living in skin tipis. They received horses in the mid-1700's. Although they lived in the midst of two other strong tribes, the Ojibwa and Cree, they were on friendly terms with them. Their greatest enemies were the Blackfeet and Gros Ventre, who lived on the western border of the Assiniboine's hunting ground. They sometimes allied with the Cree to fight the Blackfeet, Sioux, Mandan, Kutenai and Flathead.

Originally, they cremated their dead but later employed the use of the common scaffold burial. They held their Sun dance once a year but did not torture the dancers, as was common among the other tribes. They did, however, inflict self-torture upon themselves to gain strength before embarking on a war journey. They were statuesque people, who were known for the cleanliness of their villages and were visited and immortalized by the paintings of such men as George Catlin, Paul Kane, and Carl Bodmer.

Jesuit missionaries met them in 1640. They never showed any hostility to the white man. Ironically, it was the white man's disease, smallpox, which all but decimated their numbers in a series of epidemics beginning in 1780.

The Assiniboine now share two reservations in Montana with their traditional enemies—the Fort Belknap Reservation with the Gros Ventre and, with the Sioux, the Fort Peck Reservation, both of which were established in 1885.

While separate population counts do not exist, the Assiniboine number somewhere in the neighborhood of 3,000 in the United States, with possibly another 1,500 living on smaller reservations in Canada, the largest of which is the Stoney Reserve near Morley, Alberta.

The Blackfeet

The most powerful of the Algonkian-speaking tribes on the Northern Plains was the mighty Blackfeet Con-

(Smithsonian Institution)
Mehkskeme-Sukahs, a Blackfeet chief, painted in watercolor by Carl Bodmer, 1932-34.

federacy, which occupied parts of Montana and Alberta, Canada. They were divided into three independent tribes which spoke the same language—the Siksika, or Blackfeet proper, the Pikuni, or Piegan (pronounced pay-GAN), whose name refers to poorly dressed, and the Kainah, or Blood Indians. Kainah means many chiefs, but the common term Blood probably came from the Cree designation of the tribe's custom of painting their hands and bodies with red clay for certain ceremonies. The Confederacy also included the Gros Ventre, or Atsina, once a part of the Arapaho, and the Sarsi, a small Athabascan-speaking tribe from Canada.

The Blackfeet already owned horses when the first white men met them in 1750. At that time their population was estimated at 15,000.

The Blackfeet are thought to have migrated onto the Plains from the Northeast long before their neighbors. At first they lived entirely in Canada, waging war against the Flathead, Kutenai, Shoshoni, and Crow. They received European trade goods long before they ever saw a white man, through Assiniboine and Cree intermediaries. These tribes, however, soon became two of the greatest rivals of the Blackfeet.

The Blackfeet are most noted for the incessant war they waged against the early fur trappers and traders who arrived in their country in the early nineteenth century. The Blackfeet believed that the fur traders were actually allies of their hated enemies, the Crow, for it was the Crow whom the traders first met and supplied with guns. Therefore, every fur trapping party that came into their country was attacked sooner or later by Blackfeet raiding parties.

In the 1830's the Blackfeet finally accepted trade with Americans and thus began the most lucrative trade in furs ever before witnessed on the Northwestern Plains. The Blackfeet provided beaver pelts, which were in great demand in the East for men's beaver hats, and buffalo hides for coats and carriage blankets. The period 1830–1850 found the Blackfeet at the height of their power. Despite their friendliness with the American fur traders, they still kept up their warfare against other Indians on the periphery of their territory. Their power and population seemed to grow, despite two great epidemics of smallpox in 1837 and 1845. They finally made a treaty with the United States Government in 1855.

The Blackfeet were a handsome people, known for their fine arts and crafts and beautiful tipis. While other tribes wore the common eagle feather bonnets, the Blackfeet were known for their "straight up" bonnets, which were originally the insignia of a men's society called the Bulls.

Their form of the Sun dance was unlike that of other tribes, inasmuch as it centered around a woman known for her industriousness who vowed to lead the Sun dancers and who was known as the medicine woman. While she did not go through tortures, like her male counterparts in other tribes, she did participate in a number of elaborate ceremonies which preceded the actual dance. Two important ceremonies in which she presided were the Buffalo Tongues ceremony and the Sweat Lodge. Before the Sun dance, people in the camp were asked to bring buffalo tongues to a certain lodge erected for that purpose. In the lodge the tongues were ceremoniously skinned, cleaned, and boiled, then distributed to the rest of the people in camp. Later a special sweat lodge was constructed from 100 willows, which were placed in the ground and fastened at the top, like those of an ordinary sweat lodge. Participants in the Sun dance then fasted and partook of the sweat bath.

The torture ceremony was not as important to the Blackfeet as it was to some other tribes. However, there were certain men who, under duress, vowed to dance the Sun dance and torture themselves. In addition to hanging suspended from the center pole, they sometimes skewered to their backs shields and hand drums, which were ripped off after they had released themselves from the center pole. Most often the men who participated in this form of the Sun dance were leaders of war parties.

Today the Blackfeet are the second largest tribe on the Northern Plains, numbering 12,000. They live on the Blackfeet, Piegan, and Blood Reserves in Alberta and the Blackfeet Indian Reservation in Montana, consisting of nearly 1,000,000 acres. Each year tourists in Glacier National Park may visit their tipis. They still hold a Sun dance each July near Browning, Montana, and are active in other Indian events on their own and nearby reservations.

The Cheyenne

Today the Cheyenne form two groups: the Northern Cheyenne, who live on the Northern Cheyenne reservation in Montana, and the Southern Cheyenne, who live with the Southern Arapaho on land in Oklahoma. Originally, they lived together as one tribe and were first seen by white men in Minnesota in about 1640. In the Great Lakes region they lived in earth lodges and raised corn, squash, and beans, like their Arapaho neighbors. In the latter part of the seventeenth century they began their migration to the Western Plains, where they became closely associated with the Mandan, Arikara, and Hidatsa in the Upper Missouri River area. They obtained horses in about 1760 and by 1830 were full-fledged nomadic Indians, living in tipis and chasing the buffalo.

The name Cheyenne comes from the Sioux word *sahiyela,* or *sahiyena,* depending on the dialect and meaning alien speaker. Algonkian speakers, they called themselves Tsistsista, meaning the people.   .

The Cheyenne were divided into ten bands and roamed the territory now known as western Montana, eastern Wyoming, northwestern Nebraska, and part of Colorado. In 1780 their population was estimated at 3,500. After 1833 they divided into two groups, the Southern Cheyenne staying around Colorado. They fought the Kiowa, Crow, Pawnee, and Comanche and allied with the Sioux against Custer in 1876 at the Battle of the Little Big Horn.

Theirs was a history of unfortunate conflict with United States troops from 1857 to 1879. Their spirit was broken in a series of incidents, namely, the 1855 Battle of Ash Hollow and the 1864 Sand Creek Massacre, in which Colonel John M. Chivington and his troops attacked a Cheyenne camp and killed most of the people. In 1868 George Armstrong Custer attacked Chief Black Kettle's camp in the famous Battle of the Washita, killing the chief. The United States Government finally ordered the Northern Cheyenne to the Southern Cheyenne Reservation in Oklahoma. The northern Indians did not like life in the Oklahoma plains

and longed for their homeland. Finally, in the summer
of 1878, under the leadership of the Cheyenne chiefs
Dull Knife and Little Wolf, 300 Northern Cheyenne
started on the long march back to the north. They
fought all the way against United States troops who had
been ordered to force them back. When the Cheyenne
reached the north, they laid down their arms but were
ordered back to Oklahoma. In January, 1879, the Cheyenne were forced to start the long trek back through
winter blizzards. Unable to stand the biting cold, they
rebelled against the soldiers. In the fight that followed,
the haggard Cheyenne were easily beaten; 64 were
killed, 78 captured, while the rest escaped back to the

(Smithsonian Institution)
C. M. Bell took this
photo of Medicine Crow,
a Crow Indian from
Montana, in Washing-
ton, D.C., 1880. The
heavily greased pom-
padour is typical of the
Crow hair-style.

north. Later a separate reservation, then called the Tongue River Reservation, was established for the Northern Cheyenne.

Today the Northern Cheyenne Reservation has an area of 237,000 acres and is the home of approximately 3,000 Indians. About 1,500 Cheyenne live in Oklahoma on what was originally the Cheyenne-Arapaho Reservation. There is still a great deal of nomadism among the Cheyenne, and many from Montana visit their relatives in Oklahoma. Although the Cheyenne participate in the Sun dance, their most important ceremony is the Sacred Arrow Renewal. Once a year, Cheyenne from both Montana and Oklahoma gather to celebrate this important religious ceremony. The Cheyenne were particularly noted for the way in which they handled their political affairs and had an extremely well-developed judicial system.

The Crow

Tall and handsome people, the Crow Indians roamed what are now the states of Montana and North Dakota. They were owners of great herds of horses. In 1780 their population was estimated at 4,000, which is their approximate number today.

The Crow called themselves Absoraka, which referred to a small bird similar to a magpie. At one time in the past they were related to the Hidatsa of the Upper Missouri River; the tribal languages are only dialectically different. They allied themselves with the Hidatsa and Mandan and fought against the Cheyenne, Arapaho, Blackfeet, and Sioux, who often raided their territory for the purpose of capturing horses. They were friendly

Setting up tipis at the Crow Indian Fair. Even today, each Crow family attending the Fair is expected to pitch a tipi and decorate the interior in Indian fashion. This photo probably was taken in the early 1900's.

to the white man, and some Crow served as scouts for George Armstrong Custer at the Little Big Horn.

The Crow were divided into three main groups, the River Crow, Mountain Crow, and Kicked-in-their-bellies. They, in turn, were divided into thirteen clans, membership in which was inherited through the mother's side.

The Crow were known for their fine physiques and long hair, which the men combed into pompadours. Pictograph writing about the Crow always depicts this peculiar kind of hairstyle.

In addition to the Sun dance, in which a sacred doll played an important role, the Crow had elaborate ceremonies for the raising and harvesting of tobacco, and one of their most popular organizations was the Tobacco Society. They were particularly noted for their craftsmanship, and other Indians considered Crow women the most beautiful in the territory.

Today the Crow are active in a number of social events for both Indians and non-Indian tourists. They still hold their Sun dance in June, but possibly the most spectacular of their events is the Crow Indian Fair and Rodeo held near Crow Agency, Montana, in the middle of August. During the Crow Fair, each family is expected to erect a tipi. Usually more than 100 lodges are raised for this event, and the various families are judged on their ability to decorate and pitch the tipi. A number of tribes from neighboring reservations come to the fair to sing and dance and take part in the rodeo. One of the favorite songs sung with English lyrics tells about the Crow Fair:

I'll see you next summertime
Crow Indian Fair and Rodeo *hay yah yah hay yah*
We will dance the forty-nine all night long!
Way yah hah yah way yah hah yah yo!

The forty-nine is a favorite social dance for young men and women that takes place in the evening.

The Crow are also active hosts at the All-American Indian Days, held at the end of July in Sheridan, Wyo- of Miss Indian America, chosen from young girls representing most of the Western tribes. Upon being chosen

Miss Indian America, the girl spends the next year visiting various states and talking about the Indian people. The girls are chosen not only on their personality and ability, but on their awareness of their own tribal heritage. It is a beautiful sight to see all these young ladies decked out in the finest of Indian dresses to await the final decision of the panel of judges.

Living close to the Custer Battlefield National Monument, the Crow also reenact the Custer battle several times during the summer for the benefit of visiting tourists.

The Gros Ventre

The Gros Ventre, (Big Bellies) were also known as the Atsina, or Gros Ventre of the Prairie, to distinguish them from the Hidatsa of the Missouri River, who were also known as the Gros Ventre. They were a small tribe who, out of the need for protection, affiliated with the Blackfeet Confederacy. Their population was estimated at 3,000 in 1780, but a smallpox epidemic of the mid-1830's reduced their number by three-quarters. They roamed over the southern part of Saskatchewan and probably derived their name from the fact that they lived on the Big Belly River, now called the South Saskatchewan. They are considered one of the oldest residents of the Plains and are a Northern offshoot of the Arapaho, a dialect of whose language they speak.

They fought against the Assiniboine and Cree with the Blackfeet allies. Their customs and way of life were also very similar to the Blackfeet.

Today they live on the Fort Belknap Reservation in North Dakota, in which they share more than 600,000 acres with the Assiniboine. The two tribes together number more than 3,500.

The Hidatsa

Members of the Siouan language stock and linguistically related to the Crow, with whom they formed a single tribe at one time, the Hidatsa lived on the Upper Missouri River, along with their Mandan and Arikara neighbors. In 1780 their population was estimated at 2,500.

The name Hidatsa appears to refer to one of their traditional village sites which was called Village of the Willows. Their name is also sometimes translated as willow people. The Mandan called them Minitarees, which referred to their crossing the Missouri River from their original home in the East. The Crow called them Amashi, meaning earth lodges. They are now known as the Gros Ventre, the name also applied to the Atsina mentioned above.

The Hidatsa lived much like the Mandan and Arikara, dwelling in earth lodges and raising corn, squash, beans, pumpkins, and tobacco. In the middle of the eighteenth century their villages were the headquarters for the great horse trade.

They are possibly best known for their ability to trap eagles. Late in the fall the eagle trappers would build a camp a mile or so from the village. Each man would dig a pit about three feet deep, which he covered with grass and twigs to form a blind. Using a rabbit or small fox for bait, the man would climb into the pit and wait for an eagle to soar by and spot the bait. When the eagle landed on the top of the pit, the man would thrust his hands upward and grab the eagle by the legs, pulling it down into the pit and strangling it. After the feathers had been secured, there was sometimes a ceremony in which the eagle's body was buried and offerings made to its spirit.

Eagle feathers were highly prized among all the tribes of the Plains and were used both ceremoniously and as warrior insignias.

Today the Hidatsa, or Gros Ventre, as they are now commonly called, share the Fort Berthold Reservation with the Mandan and Arikara in North Dakota.

The Mandan

Mandan life of the 1830's was described in great detail by the famous painter George Catlin. He was one of the few white men who saw Mandan culture at its height before the tribe was all but decimated by small-pox epidemics which struck it in 1837.

Catlin described the Mandan as being "handsome, straight and elegant in their forms, not tall but quick and graceful, polite in their manners and neat in their persons." Because of their fairness of skin and lightness of hair, Catlin thought them to be of separate origin from the other Northern Plains tribes he visited. The Mandan were friendly and hospitable to the white man and only later signed a peace treaty with the United States in 1825 after some of their young men had become hostile.

The term Mandan appears to be a corruption of Miwatani, the name given them by the Sioux. They called themselves Numakaki, the people, and referred to themselves and their Hidatsa neighbors as Nuweta, or ourselves. They were Siouan speakers.

In 1780 their population was estimated at 3,600, but by 1804 it had decreased to less than half that number. By 1918 only 274 were left.

The Mandan lived in two fortified villages in the present state of North Dakota. Their dwellings were of the earth lodge type, ranging from forty to sixty feet in diameter. Much of their leisure time was spent lounging on the roofs of their lodges or frolicking in the nearby Missouri River. They were agriculturists and raised the usual corn, beans, squash, and tobacco. Corn was dried on the rooftops. They also made an excellent quality of pottery and basketry.

Because they were not warlike people, much of their time was spent in recreational and religious pursuits. In the center of each village they erected a large earth medicine lodge and a mysterious circular shrine made of six-foot-high panels of wood, which contained a single cedar post, said to represent the mythological spirit One Man, the brother of First Man, who in Mandan folklore was the first human being to be created.

Sacred burial grounds were located behind the villages. The Mandan were in the habit of burying their dead on scaffolds until the body disintegrated. The skulls, which were bleached white by the sun, were then taken to a special part of the cemetery and placed in a circle next to the skulls of other deceased relatives.

The Mandan form of the Sun dance, called the Okipa, was similar to the same ceremony of other tribes. But instead of being held outside, it was conducted in the central medicine lodge. The ceremony lasted for four days and was accompanied by a great deal of self-torture by men who were preparing to lead a war party or who had made special vows.

What now remains of the Mandan live on the Fort Berthold Reservation in North Dakota with the Hidatsa and Arikara.

The Plains Cree

The Plains Cree, Algonkian speakers, originally were a Woodland tribe, some of whom moved onto the Canadian Plains to hunt buffalo. The two main divisions of this tribe are thus designated Woodland Cree and Plains Cree. The name Cree is a contraction of the French form Kristineaux, the meaning of which has been lost, but which possibly referred to a name for one of the Cree bands. Because of scarcity of game in the winter, the Plains Cree often relied on hunting rabbits to the extent that their bitter enemies, the Sioux, called them Rabbit Skins. One of the most popular dances of the Sioux, learned from the Cree, is called the Rabbit dance.

Originally the Cree lived in bark wigwams, both conical and dome-shaped, and shared a culture with other Woodland tribes. As they became more adventurous, moving out onto the Plains in search of buffalo, they increasingly adopted Plains traits. By the late 1600's they were outfitted with guns and ammunition by Hudson's Bay traders, making them a terror to their enemies. They drove the Sioux out of the Great Lakes region onto the Plains. After the Cree obtained horses, their forays took them as far West as the Rocky Mountains, where they allied with the Assiniboine against the Blackfeet Confederacy. By the middle of the eighteenth century they controlled northern Manitoba and parts of Saskatchewan and Alberta. They were generally friendly to the white man.

The Cree were estimated at 4,000 strong in the 1780's, but smallpox, which struck them in 1784 and again in 1838, all but devastated their numbers.

After moving to the Plains the Cree adapted many of the customs of the Assiniboine, such as the Sun dance, but still held on to a few reminiscent of their Woodland life. They buried their dead in the ground and held an annual feast for the dead. They were particularly frightened by witchcraft and sorcery and had a ceremony in which a shaman was bound hand and foot and placed in a lone tipi. In the tipi the shaman was allegedly visited by spirits who untied him and taught him how to cure the sick or find lost objects. Sometimes, to the amazement of the devotees, the tent began to shake. Often, after being untied, the shaman was left in a ridiculous position, sometimes wedged between the tipi poles. For this reason, this particular form of religious communication has been called the Shaking Tent rite. This form of religion is still popular today on some Northern Plains reservations.

Today the Cree live on the Rocky Boy Reservation in Montana, which they share with the Ojibwa, and on various smaller reserves in Canada. They are noted especially for their ability to sing and compose most of the modern Indian songs which are heard on Plains reservations at Indian celebrations today.

The Plains Ojibwa

Like the Plains Cree, the Plains Ojibwa (Chippewa) were once part of the Woodland Chippewa, living in Wisconsin, Minnesota, Michigan, and Ontario. They moved onto the Plains in the late eighteenth century, establishing themselves as full-fledged members of the Plains tribes. The Plains Ojibwa then forsook their Woodland traits and held the Sun dance, which they had learned from their friends the Plains Cree. They had the typical warrior societies, which they called *akicita,* the same word used by the Sioux to designate the soldier societies.

The Plains Ojibwa were also called Bungi, which meant "a little bit." They called themselves Anishinabe, meaning original men, and were Algonkian speakers. In Canada they are known as the Salteaux. The word Ojibwa refers to the puckered seams of their moccasins.

The Plains Ojibwa were friendly with the Plains Cree and Assiniboine but warred against the Cheyenne, Mandan, Hidatsa, Arikara, and occasionally the Blackfeet and Sioux. In 1835 their population was estimated at 4,000. They did not fight against the white men, for there were no white settlements in their hunting land. Like the Cree, they were armed with guns and ammunition in the latter part of the 1600's.

Their customs resembled those of the Cree—a blend between the old Woodland traits and the new Plains culture. One of the most significant of the Woodland traditions was the Midewiwin, a secret religious society in which members worked up through four grades of membership. The Midewiwin shamans were often jugglers, or conjurers. There was a great belief in and dread of witchcraft. The ceremonies of the Midewiwin are still practiced today, although they are kept secret from most white men and nonmember Indians.

The Plains Ojibwa, one of the largest of the Plains

tribes, now number 7,000 on the Turtle Mountain Reservation in North Dakota. An additional 1,000 are mixed with the Cree at the Rocky Boy Reservation in Montana, and approximately 9,000 live on small reservations in Canada.

Still extremely religious people, they presented in 1959 an original Sun dance, complete with self-torture. In their form of the Sun dance each dancer pledges that he will dance for a certain number of songs. In the Turtle Mountain reenactment of the original Sun dance, dancers even dragged buffalo skulls, which had been skewered to their backs.

The Sarsi

The Sarsi (sometimes spelled Sarcee) were Athabascan speakers related to the Beaver Indians of Northern Canada. Their name translates "no good." They were an extremely small tribe, whose population in 1670 was estimated at 700 and in 1924 at 160. Because of their sparse number, they allied themselves with the Blackfeet Confederacy.

The Sarsi tribe was divided into four bands and lived north of their protectorate group in the Canadian province of Alberta. Along with the Blackfeet, they fought against the Cree and Assiniboine.

The customs of the Sarsi were similar to those of the Blackfeet. They participated in an annual Sun dance and planted tobacco, which they used ceremonially, as their single crop. They lived in tipis and took part in the Grass dance, which they received in 1833—probably from the Piegan. The Grass dance they called the Hair Parters dance and had one society by that name.

Dudwy Cle, a Sarsi Indian of Alberta, Canada, photographed by the Elliot Studio of Elmira, New York.

They also had five other societies which banded together to sponsor feasts and celebrations. Like many of the Plains tribes, the Sarsi raised dogs for ceremonial eating. This became especially popular as an accompanying ceremony of the Grass dance. However, some tribes never did indulge. Dog is still considered a great delicacy among some of the Northern Plains tribes.

Today the Sarsi live on a small tract of land south of Calgary.

The Sioux

The Sioux were—and still are—probably the best known of all Northern Plains tribes. The largest tribe of the territory, they were one of the most warlike, fighting nearly all tribes around them except the Cheyenne and Arapaho, with whom they were allied against mutual enemies. The Sioux were particularly noted for their many battles and skirmishes with United States Government troops. Most notable of these were the Battle of the Little Big Horn, sometimes erroneously called the Custer Massacre (the Sioux were defending themselves); the Fetterman Massacre; and the last official battle between American Indians and the United States Government—the Battle of Wounded Knee.

The names of great Sioux leaders have been well-recorded in American history: Red Cloud, Crazy Horse, Sitting Bull, Rain-in-the-Face, Gall, American Horse, and Young Man Afraid of His Horses. All of these men were contemporaries and led their people during the Indian wars of the 1870's.

The Sioux originally lived in the Mille Lacs region of Minnesota, where they called themselves the Oceti Sakowin, or Seven Council Fires. Each council fire represented a different tribe of the Sioux Nation: Mdewakanton, or mystery lake people; Wahpeton, or leaf people; Wahpekute, leaf shooters; Sissetonwan, or fish scale people. These four tribes were known collectively as the Isanti (usually spelled Santee), meaning "dwellers of the knife," and spoke the Sioux dialect called Dakota. This has led many people to call all of the Sioux Dakota. But this term is applied properly only to the eastern, or Santee, branch. The Ihankon and Ihanktonais (Yankton and Yanktonai) were known collectively as the Wiciyela, or middle division of Sioux, and spoke the dialect Nakota—one similar to Assiniboine. The largest division was the Teton, or western Lakota speakers, who in turn were comprised of seven tribes, the Oglala; Sicangu, or Brule; the Mnikoju;

Hunkpapa; Oohenunpa, or Two Kettle; the Itazipco, or Sans Arc; and the Sihasapa, or Blackfoot Sioux (not to be confused with the Blackfeet Confederacy).

In Minnesota the Sioux fought against the Cree and Ojibwa. The latter called them Nadowesih, signifying enemies. The French trappers who met them corrupted their name to Sioux, the name by which the tribe identifies itself today.

The western, or Teton, division began its migration onto the Western Plains after its Cree and Chippewa enemies began obtaining guns and ammunition, thus turning the tide of a series of Sioux victories. By the middle of the 18th century they were riding horses and were soon to control most of North and South Dakota, northern Nebraska, and eastern Wyoming.

Although the Sioux were friendly with the lone traders and trappers who had come to settle in their country, they began in 1849 to harass white emigrants bound for California in search of gold. Raids continued on the wagon trains until 1868, when a peace treaty was signed at Fort Laramie.

Further encroachment by the whites, however, led to what has been commonly called the Indian wars which lasted through the 1870's.

It is estimated that in 1870 the Sioux numbered 25,000. They currently live on a number of reservations in North and South Dakota, while a few live in Saskatchewan. Recent population census reports them at around 35,000, making them the second largest (to the Navajo) tribe in the United States.

3 Dwellings, Transportation, Communication

To LIVE on the Plains was to live in constant awe and respect for the elements—wind, rain, sudden dust storms, lightning, flash floods, and blizzards. The Plains Indian, by the very nature of his environment, fought a continuous battle against the forces of nature to which he attributed supernatural origins. Each day taught a new lesson in survival. But the Indian was strong and clever in combatting these daily attacks by the elements, and he adapted himself well to this rugged way of life.

The driving force behind the nomadic Plains Indian was the constant quest for food. Because he had to move around frequently to find sufficient game, he needed a kind of dwelling that provided the best protection against sudden downpours, freezing weather, and constant bombardment by the strong prairie winds. He also needed a home which could be easily dismantled and transported to the next hunting ground. The Indian had the best possible solution to this problem in the well-known tipi, possibly the best designed tent in the history of man.

Although each tribe had its own word for this conical

Typical scene on the Blackfeet Reservation, Montana, around the turn of the century. Commercially made wall tents soon replaced the traditional tipi. Horse-and-wagon became the modern Indian conveyance.

dwelling, the word tipi, sometimes spelled "teepee," is a Sioux word meaning "they dwell" and was used generically to indicate this kind of tent. The Sioux today use the word tipi to designate any kind of dwelling. When they refer to the conical tipi, the call it *ikcetipi,* or original tipi.

The tipi was constructed in basically two designs. The Sioux, Cheyenne, Arapaho, Assiniboine, Mandan, Arikara, Gros Ventre, and Plains Cree used a tipi in which three poles formed the basic support. The Crow, Blackfeet, Hidatsa, and Sarsi constructed their tipis using a four-pole support. The three-pole support gave the tipi the appearance of being tilted slightly forward, while the four-pole design made it perpendicular to the ground. Of the two, the three-pole support was the stronger, partially because after the rest of the poles had been stacked against the tripod, they were lashed together where they joined. Most of the poles were placed in the forward crotches of the tripod, giving it the appearance of being front-heavy. In the four-pole design, the poles were simply laid against the supports, without being lashed.

Before the arrival of the horse on the Plains, tipis were smaller so that they could easily be carried by a dog. Only ten or twelve poles were needed to erect this smaller lodge. After horses became available, tipis grew larger, often being made from as many as twenty-five buffalo skins supported by sixteen or more poles.

The tipi was the perfect home. It could be rolled up and packed and carried from one camping area to the next with little difficulty. It stood up well under the severest weather conditions because of its particular shape and design, and it provided a warm home in the winter and an easily ventilated one in the summer.

Erecting the tipi was the duty of the woman, and it was usually considered her personal property. Ideally the poles were made from lodge pole pine, but yellow pine and cedar were also used. The poles ranged from twenty to twenty-five feet in length among the Sioux and as long as forty feet among the Crow, giving the latter's tipi the appearance of an hourglass. Smaller tipis using shorter poles were used by hunters for overnight camping, and play tipis were constructed by children, much as a non-Indian child makes a playhouse.

Women selected and tanned buffalo hides to make the tipi cover. The hides were sewn together to form

(Smithsonian Institution)

Interior of a Blackfeet tipi at Heart Butte, Montana, in 1951. The old woman is rocking a baby to sleep in a blanket hammock suspended from the tipi poles.

roughly a half circle, allowing for the "ears," or smoke flaps, and a circular opening, which became the doorway. The door itself was made from a separate buffalo hide, which could be hung over the opening when the owners were away. This was an admonition for people to stay out.

When a new tipi had been sewn, it could be painted in a variety of designs using native earth colors for paint and special bones for brushes. Usually several pitched in to paint the tipi cover. Pictograph drawings, representing the war deeds of the master of the house, were often painted on the cover. The pictographs showed how the owner went on the warpath or raided horses, in a series of near-realistic drawings leading around the circumference of the tipi. Some tipis were painted according to visions the owner had received. Usually these symbolic designs appeared on the larger medicine lodges, representing clouds or eagles, buffalo, or other animals which had been inspired supernaturally.

To erect the tipi, the women first placed the three or four poles together to form a basic support. These were raised into position, and the balance of the poles were laid against the crotches formed by the support. The tipi cover was then tied to the back, or raising, pole, and lifted into position against the back of the framework. The cover was unrolled over the framework until it met at the doorway. It was then laced together in front with special lacing pins, and stones were placed around the bottom to hold the cover to the ground. When the camp was moved, these stones were left in place, forming tipi rings, remnants of which can still be seen today on the Western Plains.

A particular characteristic of the raised tipi was the tipi ears, or smoke flaps, which were on either side of the smoke hole, held in place by two poles. They could be adjusted to control the smoke inside and closed in case of a sudden shower.

Hunters away from the camp for only a few nights did little more than pitch a small tipi and use their buffalo robes for bedding. When the band made camp for a few weeks, however, great pains were taken to make the interior of the tipi as comfortable as possible. The women placed an inner lining called dew cloth around the inside of the tipi, reaching from the ground upward as high as six feet. It was secured in place by tying it to a rope spaced between the lodge poles. The dew cloth served to keep out the dampness and chill winds and also helped regulate the draft of air. It was often painted in geometric designs or pictographs, like the tipi cover. Some elaborate dew cloths were decorated with beadwork and quillwork, making the interior of the tipi very colorful.

The fireplace, which served as the cooking area in wintertime, was dug directly below the smoke hole. In the summer the cooking was done outdoors, often in a separate arbor of small pine trees. Around the fireplace, extending back to the dew cloth, the women laid buffalo robes, deer skins, and other fur pelts to form a soft and cozy floor for the tipi. Each member of the family had his own special place in the tipi where he kept his extra clothes, personal belongings, and sleeping robe. Backrests made of willows were placed around the sides for comfortable sitting. Small utensils, personal effects, and dried meat were kept in colorfully painted containers called parfleches. The parfleches were made of raw buffalo hides, which were painted in geometric designs and fashioned into boxes or envelopes. They, in essence, served as dresser drawers and suitcases for the Plains Indian and could easily be packed and transported. A special cylindrical rawhide case was used to store the man's warbonnet. Beaded or quilled pouches and saddlebags were also used for storing and packing and preservation of ceremonial objects.

When the Indians built a permanent winter camp, they often constructed brush windbreaks around the tipi, as an additional measure to keep out the strong winter winds. Sometimes they made dome-shaped inner linings inside the tipi in case of extreme cold. This inner lodge—not to be confused with the dew cloth—helped concentrate the heat from the fire and keep out drafts. In the summer the tipi could easily be ventilated by rolling up the cover and letting the cool winds blow through.

The warrior of the lodge usually kept his weapons on a small tripod outside the doorway of the tipi, where they would be ready for him in case of a surprise attack by the enemy. Next to the tipi the women constructed frames of saplings, on which they hung strips of meat to dry in the sun.

Normally, when the bands were separated from one another, the tipis were pitched close together for protection against the elements and enemies. However, once a year when the bands assembled for the Sun dance, the tipis were arranged in a large circle. Often, in the center of the circle was a council lodge. A large lodge was usually constructed by placing two tipis close together and joining the covers. These lodges were used for council meetings of the headmen of the different bands, or sometimes for celebrations sponsored by the warrior societies and dance clubs. The placement of the tipis was usually under the direction of these warrior societies, who received their orders from the council chiefs.

The Sun dance camp was greatly anticipated by the Indian people, for there they could renew old acquaintances and make new ones. Although there was an air of sacredness about the Sun dance, there was plenty of time for dancing and feasting and meeting with friends. This might be the only time during the year when friends from different bands could see one another. It was also a time when the young men courted the young women of their fancy.

The Indian people were very modest, and courtship was done in secret. Usually a young brave would wait for his sweetheart along a path she took to get water from a nearby stream. When she appeared, he might throw a pebble at her to attract her attention, or tug at her sleeve as she passed by. If she liked him, she would stop and talk for a few moments. If not, she would pass by without noticing him. Young men often composed love songs, which they played on flutes a distance away from their sweethearts' tipis.

If marriage was agreed upon, the parents of the engaged couple exchanged gifts. The man usually had to prove that he was a good hunter and fearless warrior, while the young girl had to show her proficiency in cooking and making clothing. When the marriage was announced, the women got together to make the new tipi for the married couple.

There were many activities at the Sun dance camp exclusive of the religious ceremony itself. There was much feasting and dancing. Warrior societies might challenge one another to ball games or feats of skill. Children dashed in and around the lodges, playing games, while older boys raced their horses around the circle of tipis. The old people took the opportunity to exchange news and gossip and reminisce about Sun dances of long ago.

In the middle of the nineteenth century, buffalo hides began to become scarce. Not only were the great buffalo

A Rosebud Sioux couple in front of their log cabin. Bell Photo.
(Courtesy John Colhoff)

herds diminishing, but Indians were beginning to obtain canvas, which made a perfect substitute. The new canvas tipis were light, easily transportable, and, because of this, could be made larger. The canvas tipis were painted and erected in the same manner as their hide predecessors, but were more uniform in design.

After the Indians were forced to live on reservations, tipis began to be replaced by wall tents—many of which were made on the reservations. The Indians were also encouraged to build permanent homes—mostly log cabins in the early period, and, later, frame houses.

Many Indian families pitched tents and tipis near their permanent homes and used them as extra bedrooms during the summer months. Occasionally, poor people lived in wall tents the year around. During the early 1900's and even through the 1940's, the typical permanent home of an Indian family consisted of a one-room log or frame structure, a wall tent, or tipi, and, in most areas, an additional shade of pine boughs, in which the Indian women did their cooking in the summertime. Today this shade is sometimes jokingly referred to as the squaw cooler by the Indians themselves.

Since the 1950's there has been an effort by the United States Government to establish better housing on the Indian reservations. One now sees housing developments in Indian country, but for the most part Indians still have inadequate, small homes.

Despite the increase of frame houses and other permanent homes, tipis still survive today. While a scattering may be found on practically all reservations, none can compare with the tipis of the Crow and Blackfeet, which are still pitched at their annual summer encampments. During the Crow Indian Fair, for instance, more than 100 tipis are raised each year. The Crow take great pride in their tipis, and each year prizes are awarded to the family that brings the best-looking one.

Another type of Plains dwelling used by the Mandan, Hidatsa, and Arikara was called the earth lodge.

Earth lodges were large circular or octagonal structures, averaging forty feet in diameter. They were constructed by erecting forked poles around the circular or octagonal circumference, which were, in turn, con-

(Smithsonian Institution)
Mandan earth lodge used for ceremonies. Photo by F. B. Fiske.

nected by crosspieces. A square framework of poles was erected in the center to serve later as the smoke hole and cooking place. The upright poles around the circumference were reinforced with diagonally placed buttresses, and the entire framework was connected by willows and mattings of willow and grass, which were covered with a veneer of mud, making it water- and windproof. The doorway, or entrance corridor, was about ten feet long and could be closed by means of a rawhide door.

The interior of the earth lodge was divided into sleeping compartments and the central cooking area; it could house several families. Sometimes owners provided space inside the earth lodge for favorite horses overnight.

An earth lodge village contained anywhere from 30 to 200 such lodges. The villages were fortified by

This dog travois was made by Black Horse, a Cheyenne from Lame Deer, Montana, at the request of Thomas M. Galey, who took the photo around 1922. Black Horse's wife poses with the travois.

trenches and stockades and were usually located on high promontories for additional safety. In the center of each village was an earth medicine lodge used for religious ceremonies. It was constructed in a similar manner but was twice as large as the normal dwelling. Because of their locations and fortifications, these villages were impenetrable. The only way hostile Indians could attack those who lived there was to draw them out by keeping the buffalo away.

The dog, and later the horse, was truly the camel of the Plains. During the summer months—or for large portions of them—the Indians lived in semi-permanent villages at the Sun dance sites. But during most of the year it was necessary to move the camp from place to place in search of game. Rarely did entire tribes come together except for the Sun dance. When an entire camp was on the move, all tipis and personal belongings were placed on the animals' backs or on travois made for the dogs and horses. A travois was a V- or X-shaped structure. One end was attached to the back of a dog or horse, while the free ends dragged on the ground. Sometimes a carrier was lashed between the poles in which young babies or the very old or infirm rode. Usually the women rode travois horses.

Young babies spent most of their early days strapped to a cradleboard, which could be easily hung on a saddle horn when the family was on the move. When the mother was busy in the tipi, the cradleboard could be hung in a tree, where the gentle breeze would rock the baby to sleep.

Before moving camp, the headmen held a council to decide the direction the people were to follow. Some of the war societies were chosen to act as rear and flank guards, while others went ahead to serve as scouts. Normally it was the responsibility of the women to pack the belongings onto travois and horses and move the camp. The men carried only their weapons in case of a surprise attack by hostile tribes. Advance scouts might travel as far as two or three miles ahead of the rest of the people.

The number of horses each family owned largely determined the size of its tipi and amount of personal belongings, for it took a number of horses to move a single lodge and its furnishings. John C. Ewers, a lead-

A Blackfeet horse travois photographed around 1900. The very young, old, or infirm were carried on the travois when the camp moved.

ing expert on the Blackfeet, estimates that the weight of the usual Blackfeet lodge and its furnishings averaged 560 to 585 pounds, requiring three horses to bear the entire weight. The poles were dragged from each side of one or two horses, while the tipi cover was folded and usually placed between the horns of the saddle. Mules were preferred to horses, because they could carry heavier loads than the small Indian ponies. If a man had no horses, he could often borrow them from a man wealthier than he. Or he might have to resort to moving all his belongings on the backs of dogs.

Distance traveled by the moving camp averaged ten to fifteen miles per day. The ideal stopover place had shelter from the elements, as well as good grass for the horses. During the winter a camp was usually made in a wooded area, away from the winds of the open prairie. The tipis were pitched close together to afford additional protection. Only in summer encampments, where all the bands of the tribes assembled, were the tipis pitched in a large circle. In such a camp, a favorite horse might be tied near the owner's home, but usually the horses were put out to pasture under the watchful eyes of young boys. It was during this time that horse raiders from other tribes might try their luck running off the picketed horses.

Crossing a stream provided some difficulty. Usually

A Hidatsa bullboat in the collection of the National Museum, Washington, D.C. Made from rawhide stretched over a wooden frame, bullboats were used to cross large streams and rivers.

(Smithsonian Institution)

the travois and tipi poles were lashed together to form a raft. The horses were ridden through the water; often the men and boys hung on the tails of the horses as they swam to the opposite shore. Many streams and rivers were nearly dry and could be easily forded at a shallow place.

The Mandan, Hidatsa, and Arikara used a boat called a bullboat made from a buffalo hide stretched over a circular frame of saplings resembling a large washtub. It was propelled by means of a single paddle. A bullboat could easily be carried by a woman. When not in use, it was usually stored on the roof of the owner's earth lodge. It was especially useful in crossing the Missouri River.

Eastern divisions of the Plains Indians, such as the Santee Dakota, the Plains Cree, and Ojibwa used the popular birch bark canoe. The Plains Ojibwa also used a two-wheel cart called the red river cart, which was modeled after a European design. The carts were drawn by both horses and oxen.

The nomadic drive came to a sad decline after the Indians were confined to reservations. While they could occasionally obtain permission to leave the reservation to go on buffalo hunts, white officials encouraged them to settle down and live off the annuities provided by the Federal Government. Each week beef, flour, sugar, and other commodities were distributed to the Indian families. The distribution center was the agency, the home of the Indian agent and field office of the United States Government. Agency towns soon became the focal point of activity.

Still holding allegiance to band leaders, the Indians

settled down on allotments of land. These band remnants soon developed into smaller towns. In order to travel from their homes to the agency, the Indian soon adapted to the horse-and-wagon.

It was common to see the typical horse-and-wagon of the Indians even in the 1950's. It was the main mode of transportation from their scattered homes to the agency on Saturday mornings, when they picked up their annuities or made stops at the local traders and stores. During the Sun dance, families moved their tents and belongings to the central site by wagon. One saw old-timers and their wives riding high on the wagon seat, with the rest of their family and equipment packed behind. Sometimes a favorite riding horse was tied to the back of the wagon and led to the Sun dance grounds. The creaking wagon wheels cut deep networks of roads across the reservations and later became the highways of automobile travel.

By the mid-1950's the box wagons had largely been replaced by the automobile. Reservation roads were soon paved, major highways bisecting some of them. Being poor, the Indians bought secondhand cars, which they jestingly referred to as Indian cars. Soon, just as Indians had become masters of the horse, they became masters of the automobile. Now the Indians could travel faster and farther to visit relatives and friends on adjoining reservations. And, like the horse, the automobile had a great influence on Indian culture.

From this quick mode of travel and increasing Indian interest in their own traditions, there grew a movement called Pan-Indianism. Pan-Indianism has often been called an attempt to unify all the Indian tribes. It is most dramatic in its arts and crafts and music and dance. Because the Indians travel from reservation to reservation with ease, there has been a widespread diffusion of customs, songs, dances, and costume styles. In some areas it is difficult to determine the tribe by the manner of dress nowadays, especially at the many powwows held throughout the Western reservations.

The automobile created a new mechanical language. Today it is common to see two Indian mechanics talking about the intricacies of the automobile engine in their own native language.

Old customs survive with modern connotations. Once, for example, I attended the Pine Ridge Sioux Sun dance and witnessed an unusual custom, one blending the old and new. My family and I were camped in a tipi overlooking the Sun dance grounds. At about five in the morning I was startled out of a deep sleep by the sound of a huge drum being beaten outside the tipi. I quickly dressed and opened the tipi flap to see a group of young men carrying a drum and making their way to the next tent. They stopped in front of the tent and one of them, the leader, began a speech in Sioux, telling the people that they had traveled a long way and were trying to earn gas money for the return trip. A sleepy woman opened the tent flap and asked that they sing a song honoring a relative who had been killed in battle. Immediately the singers started up a song, and the woman danced in the doorway of her tent in time to the rhythmic precision of the drum. When they had finished the song, she handed them some change. They thanked her and started for the next tent, making their way to every tent in the village.

Long ago this custom had been observed whenever a warrior society wanted to go out and sing. They would "beg" for food and gifts from people in the village. What had once been called the Begging dance, is now called Doorway or, as the Sioux call it, They dance in the doorway. The main purpose for the revival of this custom is to raise money to buy gas. Thus, the old and new are blended in typical Indian fashion.

There were a variety of ways in which Indians used to communicate across the large expanses of land. It was often necessary to send signals from far away in order to warn of enemy tribes in the vicinity or of the proximity of game.

One of the most common and well-known techniques was the smoke signal. This was effected by building a small fire of green wood and placing a damp robe or blanket over it. The blanket was then lifted off the fire quickly, producing a puff of smoke. The signals were predetermined. One puff of smoke might mean enemies were near; two puffs, buffalo, and so on.

Signals were also sent by means of small signal mirrors traded from the white men. Again, a certain number of flashes indicated the presence of enemies or game. This method, of course, could be used only on sunny days and was somewhat limited.

Scouts were usually told to report what they found as soon as they discovered it. A scout often carried a blanket with him, which he waved in certain ways to indicate that he had found buffalo. A returning war party might signal with the blanket before arriving in camp to indicate whether or not the war journey had been successful.

A buffalo scout might run back to camp in a zigzag course, indicating that he had found buffalo. Guns were fired to alert the village if enemies were approaching.

Probably the best communication developed and used exclusively by the Plains Indian was sign language. Sign language, or hand gesture language, was the universal parlance of the Plains tribes.

Because the tribes had no written language, sign language was not like the deaf and dumb sign language which basically has one sign for each letter of the alphabet, plus signs for complete words which are used a great deal. Indian sign language employed one sign for one word or concept. Refined as a trade language between alien peoples, it was nevertheless very simple; compared with spoken languages of the Plains, it had an extremely limited vocabulary.

Sign language was logical; you would find much of it intelligible without ever seeing it before. Placing both hands in front of you at chest level with palms parallel to the ground and moving one in front of the other would indicate walking. Moving them rapidly would mean running. Raising your right hand over your head and slightly in front, with your palm facing downward, would indicate tall (we use the same sign ourselves), while placing it below your waist with palm down meant short. To move your index finger forward meant go; to pull it back to you signified come. Colors and objects to trade were usually pointed to, although common objects such as horse, coffee, tobacco, and other popular commodities, had special signs.

Abstract concepts were very limited. Power was signified by making the sign for strong. Evil simply became bad. Knowledge was indicated by the sign for know.

Like many Europeans, Indians usually talked with their hands even when speaking their own language. When in camp, they could talk to one another at long distances, without ever having to shout, by using signs. An important message could be delivered to someone engrossed in conversation without ever interrupting. It was especially useful in warfare, when a spoken command might lead to a war party's discovery by the enemy.

Even though most Indians speak and understand English today, sign language has not died out. One can still see old-timers from different tribes talking together, their hands moving rapidly in enthusiastic conversation.

In modern times Indian languages have proved to be an invaluable code during wartime. During the First and Second World Wars and the Korean War, many of the Indian languages were used by radio teams whose members were of the same tribe. While normally even the most complicated code can eventually be broken, it was impossible for the enemy ever to break through the American Indian language barrier.

4 The Quest for Food

For those of us living in contemporary American
society dominated by shopping centers and supermarket
chains, restaurants and delicatessens, it is difficult to
imagine one having to go out and hunt in order to survive. It is also hard to fathom just how much time one
would have to spend in search of food—locating it,
killing it, skinning it, and, finally, preparing it. But such
was the lot of the Plains Indian.

In the Plains Indian society the everyday jobs of men
and women were clearly defined, and much of the distribution of labor was similar to our own. The Indian
men were providers. Providing food and clothing meant
continual hunting—matching wits with buffalo, elk,
antelope, and deer; meeting them in their own habitat;
and finding the most effective way to kill them. Women
attended to the domestic chores—the making and keeping of the house, preparing and cooking the food, making and decorating the clothing for the entire family.
The Plains economy was essentially based on the ability
of men to provide.

After the Indians were put on reservations, there developed many misconceptions about them, such as that

68

they are shiftless and lazy. This is untrue. What we must remember is that after the Indians settled on reservations, the men were deprived of their one main occupation: hunting. The buffalo had diminished, and food allotments replaced the usual game diet. Hunting was not replaced with other jobs. Therefore, the Indian men were left with no occupations while the women still performed their household chores. This gave rise to the popular opinion that Indian women do all the work.

Today, jobs are few on the reservations. Many Indians earn a living by leasing their land to white ranchers and farmers, but most are unemployed. Recently the government has been attempting to lure industry onto reservations in order to provide Indians with jobs without their having to leave their homes, but jobs are still scarce.

In ancient times, before the white man and the horse, the Indian was actively employed in his daily quest for food. As he adapted his dwellings and methods of transportation to the severity of Plains life, he also developed unusual hunting techniques.

The main weapons used for hunting were the bow and arrow. Early arrows were tipped with flint or bone heads. while iron points were later obtained from traders. The bow was accurate only at close range, so it was necessary for the hunter to approach his game closely, taking careful aim and trying to down or wound the animal on the first shot. A miss would surely frighten the game away. In order to get close enough to an animal, the Indian hunter had to approach it from the downwind side, or the animal would pick up the human scent. Often the hunter wore the skin of a wolf or buffalo so that he might approach his game without being discovered until he was close enough to let an arrow fly. Often two men would conceal themselves in the skin of a buffalo and meander close to the herd. A third man hiding behind the other two would then leap out and shoot his quarry.

In the winter camps, made up of small bands of hunters, only a few men might go out in search of game, following their tracks in the snow or waiting in silence in the snowbanks for an unsuspecting straggler of a buffalo separated from his herd. It was sometimes so cold that the hunters had to dig holes or caves in the snow, where they crawled to keep warm. The hunters might be accompanied by dogs that carried the fresh meat on back packs.

During the summer the entire village might participate in a buffalo hunt. Naturally, before the coming of the horse, Indians had to hunt on foot. Stampeding the animals over cliffs was one of the primary ways of hunting buffalo before they were chased on horseback.

There were certain "runs" on the Plains which were used each year to stampede buffalo. When a buffalo herd had been sighted by the scouts, the people grabbed blankets and buffalo robes and formed two lines. Other Indians with robes lined up behind the buffalo and began waving their robes and yelling. Sometimes the prairie around the herd was set on fire. The frightened buffalo began to stampede between the two lines of Indians, who, in turn, waved their robes and yelled to keep the buffalo between them. The lane between the lines led to a steep precipice. At this point the buffalo were running so fast that the lead buffalo could not stop, and the herd hurled itself over the cliff, most of it being killed in the fall. Those that were only wounded were shot with arrows or clubbed to death by hunters waiting at the foot of the cliff. The buffalo then were skinned and butchered by the women at the bottom of the cliff, and their meat was packed on dogs for the trip back to camp.

A variation of this hunting technique was called the buffalo pound. The same idea of chasing the buffalo between two lines of people was used, but in this case they were driven into a corral, where they were shot with arrows and clubbed. Although primitive and crude, these techniques of buffalo hunting were perfect for the terrain and the weapons at hand. Only after the introduction of the horse were these methods abandoned.

The horse radically changed the Indians' technique of hunting, for the buffalo could be chased and killed on the run. Buffalo hunting now became a challenging sport, a test of the hunter's prowess as a rider and marksman.

The summer, when buffalo were easy to find, was the season for the great tribal buffalo hunts. The camps followed the herds until scouts found them and came back to report to the headmen of the village. The people prepared their weapons, and the warrior societies were summoned to keep order during the buffalo hunt.

The hunters, always ready to display individual prowess, often left the main body of hunters and attacked the herd single-handed. In most cases this would frighten away the remaining buffalo, and the rest of the hunters would not get their chance to kill any. The headmen thus restricted hotheaded individuals by having the group of hunters policed by the warrior societies. If a hunter broke ranks and tried to reach the buffalo before the rest of the main body, he would be severely attacked by the warrior policeman. Such an offense called for his weapons to be broken, for him to be beaten with the back of a bow, or sometimes for his tipi to be slashed, as a reminder. There were cases when such an offender was killed, but this was done in justification of those who might go without food should the buffalo be frightened away.

When the signal was given, the hunters galloped their ponies into the thundering herd of buffalo. Each man singled out his animal and, riding very close, killed it with arrows. Charging into a herd this way was dangerous business. The buffalo pony had to be particularly well-trained, for at any moment the buffalo might turn his head and hook the horse and rider with its powerful horns. Urging his pony forward with knees and feet and riding without saddle, the rider approached the buffalo from the right side and let his arrow fly into the fatal area just behind the foreleg. He would then quickly reach into his quiver, notch another arrow, and shoot again. If a hunter was particularly efficient—or just lucky—he might down the buffalo with one arrow, but normally it took several arrows to do the job. Even then the buffalo often had to be clubbed to death.

Lances were sometimes used. A rider would approach the buffalo with a raised lance and stab it until it dropped. Very rarely was the lance thrown.

Bows and arrows remained the preferred weapons even after the Indians obtained guns. The early muzzle-loaders could not be reloaded easily on the run. Later, breech-loaders were obtained from traders, but they were never in great quantity.

Although the buffalo chase was a challenging and exciting sport, the hunter often lost his life beneath the trampling hooves. Ponies might step in a prairie doghole, tumbling the rider into the herd.

The women followed the hunters, leading packhorses, and quickly began to skin and butcher the buffalo. Each buffalo was marked with the hunter's arrow or marker stick, which could readily be identified by his female relatives. The meat was packed in the skin of the buffalo and carted back to camp on the horses' backs or on travois. The meat of a buffalo averaged about 400 pounds, so it took several horses to carry the entire carcass. Choice bits of buffalo meat—the tongue, kidneys, and liver—were often eaten on the spot.

Boys were taught to hunt by their male relatives as soon as they learned to walk. They were given small bows and blunt-headed arrows, with which they were encouraged to hunt birds and small animals. In this way they developed marksmanship and experienced the thrill of the hunt at a very young age. They were constantly reminded by their adult companions that the future of their people would be decided by their ability to succeed as hunters and providers. As the boys grew older their fathers and uncles took them on the buffalo hunts, where they singled out calves and shot them. This was excellent training with less risk for a boy. The boy who shot his first buffalo calf was feasted by the entire camp and his name proclaimed by the camp herald. By the time he had reached his early teens he was ready for the real buffalo hunt. The quicker he could prove him-

Cheyenne Indians drying meat on racks in 1895. Large intestines were cleaned and filled with blood to make blood sausage.

self a reliable hunter, the sooner he would be able to participate in all the activities of the male adults in camp and discard his boyhood status.

Girls also received training in domestic chores by their mothers, aunts, and grandmothers when they were very young. They were taught to make dolls and miniature tipis and played house Indian-style. They also learned the art of decoration from the older women. Just as the boys were taught to be providers, the girls were taught that they must be industrious. If they were not, young warriors never would marry them.

To augment their supply of meat, the Plains Indians also picked a variety of wild plums and chokecherries, which they ate raw or dried and made into a sweet soup.

Often these chokecherries were pounded together with meat and fat in what is commonly called pemmican. Hunters and warriors who were away from the camp for several days often carried sacks of pemmican as their only food. It was nourishing, would not spoil, and did not have to be cooked.

Meat was usually boiled or roasted. For a kettle, the Indians used a paunch made of buffalo. It was either placed in a hole in the ground or suspended from a tripod. It was filled with water and hot stones until the water boiled, then the meat was added. This quick-boiling method of cooking is still found on reservations today, but the paunches have been replaced by iron kettles, and the cooking is done on gas or electric stoves.

In a culture where refrigeration was unknown, a method had to be developed to preserve food. The average buffalo yielded about 400 pounds of meat; while much of it was eaten soon after the hunt, some had to be stored for future use. Meat which was not immediately consumed was cut into small thin strips and hung on a framework of saplings to dry in the sun. This kind of meat is called jerky, and it could be kept indefinitely. It was tough to eat, but very tasty.

Another staple on the Plains was the Indian turnip, which grew in the hills. It was gathered by women who dug it up by means of a special digging stick. The turnips were woven together by their stems and hung to dry until needed. Then they were boiled.

In North Dakota among the Mandan, Hidatsa, and Arikara, agriculture was highly developed. While the tribes hunted buffalo and smaller game in the winter, their main staples were corn, beans, squash, and pumpkins, which they raised in small five- to six-acre gardens in their fortified villages. These garden products were traded with other tribes for horses, robes, and fresh meat.

The major crops were planted in the spring and harvested in October. First the garden spots were raked over with rakes made of sticks or deer antlers. Often, brush was laid over the ground and burned to loosen the soil. Table scraps provided fertilizer. The ground was broken with hoes made from the shoulder blades of buffalo and, later, iron. The seeds were planted by making a hole with a pointed digging stick and dropping the kernels in. Young children were stationed in the gardens to keep birds and insects away from the crops.

The corn was boiled or roasted and eaten on the cob or made into corn cakes. Dried corn was hung inside the lodges or stored in underground caches.

The Eastern Sioux and the Plains Ojibwa and Cree supplemented their meat diet with wild rice, which they collected from their birchbark canoes, and fish, which were caught either on bone hooks or in traps.

Once placed on reservations, the Indians were introduced to new foods. The government provided them with beef, which at first the Indians disliked because of its foul smell. The government planned to make farmers out of all the Plains Indians but failed when the Indians would not "scratch the soil" with plows. Other staples, like sugar, flour, and pork, were also provided. The Indians had never seen flour before and threw away the contents so that they might use the flour sacks for clothing. Later they were taught how to make bread. One of the favorite dishes that survives today is called Indian bread, or fried bread, which is made of fluffy dough fried in deep fat. It is an important part of every traditional Indian meal today.

Although the idea is somewhat repulsive to non-Indians (and even to some Indians, notably the Blackfeet and Crow) many of the Northern Plains tribes ate dogmeat. Usually the eating of dog—considered a delicacy—was connected with a religious feast. Small puppies were often strangled and cooked with the hair left on. The hair was then removed and the choice parts boiled and eaten. Often, there were elaborate ceremonies which accompanied the eating of dog. Many of these ceremonies became widespread along with a dance called the Grass dance, which became diffused among the Northern Plains tribes in the latter part of the nineteenth century. Today, eating dog is still common on many of the Northern Plains reservations, where young puppies are raised especially for the occasion. Many of the other Indians living along the periphery of the Plains area contemptibly refer to the Northern Indians as dog eaters.

Once I attended an Indian celebration, accompanied by an old man. During the course of the dance, when the dancers had stopped to eat, he asked me to join him. He handed me a rather large leg of meat and said, "Chicken." I began to eat, but it tasted like no chicken I had ever eaten before. When I inquired whether he was sure it was chicken, he chuckled and replied, "Dog!"

As a breeder of dogs back home, I was hesitant to finish the meal. But not wanting to disappoint my host, I finished the leg and made up my mind never to make the same mistake again. My host was very pleased.

The Plains Indians made a variety of cooking utensils

of wood and bone. Buffalo horns served as ladles. Meat and soup were eaten from wooden dishes. Hot coals were handled with wooden paddles, and water was kept in bags made of buffalo paunches. The traders introduced the Indians to metal knives and axes and iron kettles, which were always in great demand. Flint and steel from the traders replaced the primitive fire drill.

The reservation system was designed to crush the Indians' traditional economy and turn them into white men. But the Indian had a different concept about the land he lived on. The government drew up a plan to allot each Indian family a section of land, which that family would learn to farm and on which they could raise cattle and sheep. In no time, the government thought, the Indian would be assimilated into the mainstream of white culture, raising crops, irrigating their land, and tending their cattle. But the Indian had never thought of the land as something that could be sliced up into sections and given to one man to own. The traditional Indian economy was basically a communal one, and what the tribe owned belonged to all the members.

There was a great deal of emphasis placed on farming, yet this was a concept completely foreign to most tribes. True, some of them were successful at raising crops in limited numbers for the consumption of individual families, with some left over to trade to non-agricultural peoples. But none of the Plains tribes depended solely on crops for its diet. Fresh meat in camp was still to them the sign of abundance.

The land alloted as Indian reservations did not lend itself particularly well to farming. Most of the reservation areas contained dry, barren land, not easily manageable. Furthermore, while the government provided Indians with plows and other farming equipment, there was never much concern about teaching the Indian people to actually use this equipment. Many of the farm tools rusted away during the severe winters.

The Indians became dependent on the annuities provided by the government. True, they could still hunt on their reservation lands (many still do), but how much easier it was, especially in the severe winters, to simply collect the foodstuffs provided by the government through treaty obligations.

In the beginning, beef was distributed on the hoof. Once a week, on what was to be known as Distribution Day, Indian families left their homes and traveled by horse-and-wagon to the distribution centers. The cattle, after being driven in, would be penned up in a corral. As each Indian head of household was called, a bull was let out through the chute, and the Indian chased the animal out onto the prairie with bow and arrow or rifle to shoot his beef on the run. The Indians enjoyed this immensely, as it was reminiscent of the old buffalo hunting days. When the bull had been killed, the Indian women would follow and butcher the animal and pack the meat in the wagon for the long trip home. Distribution Day also became a time when old friends could get together and exchange gossip and talk of the old times. There would also be singing and dancing until the slaughtering and butchering were over and it was time to head home.

Because of the Indians' affinity to horses and the methods of beef distribution, it is not surprising that many of the young Indian men became interested in the cowboy's life. Several went to work as ranch hands for neighboring white men, an occupation still enjoyed today by many Indians. Rodeos became popular, and the Indians became proficient in bronco riding, roping, and bulldogging. Today there are many all-Indian and smaller tribal rodeos on all Plains reservations.

While most Indians had no training or interest in farming and ranching, many allowed white ranchers and farmers to come in and lease their land. Today the prime income of Northern Plains Indians is through land lease.

As the Indians became more settled, communities began to develop on the reservations. Traders, many of them descendants of the original Indian traders, moved in and established trading posts in the small communities. At the trading post the Indian could buy foodstuffs, clothing, and other daily needs. More likely than not, ready cash was not available to the Indian, but he did have collateral in his land lease money. Traders therefore started a credit system, the Indian purchasing his needs at the store and signing a voucher to be paid to the trader when he received his lease money. The credit system is still an important aspect of Indian trading.

In addition to credit, the Indian often pawned or traded beadwork or other craftwork with the trader in exchange for commodities. As a result, traders often went into the Indian arts and crafts business, a major source of income for many.

Many of the trading post customers were old-time Indians who had never learned or preferred not to speak English. It is not uncommon, even today, to find white traders who can at least do business in native Indian languages. The trading posts themselves have changed little since they first flourished on the reservations and around the forts. They still carry the same line of boots, saddles, Western hats and clothing, foodstuffs, fresh meat, and ice-cold soda pop for the children. In the smaller communities the trading post is the center of civil activity, and the porch is usually lined with old Indian men and women, exchanging gossip and watching amusedly the tourists who visit Indian country. Often the local post office and gasoline station is part of the total trading post operation and is in essence the business center of each reservation community.

Today, shopping centers and restaurants are cropping up on all Indian reservations. The Indian has become conscious of brands, partially due to television commercials which find their way into a minority of Indian homes. But basically the Indians' attitude toward sharing their food with those who cannot provide for themselves is like it was in the buffalo hunting days. The high point of any Indian celebration is the mass distribution of free food to singers, dancers, and spectators. At all the major dances, whole beefs and other staples are donated to the sponsoring committee, and the food is prepared communally, usually over open fires, and distributed to the masses of people in attendance. An important part of any Indian's powwow equipment is a sack of eating utensils, which he carries religiously to the dance grounds. At each meal the people are told by an announcer to get their dishes and line up for the distribution of food. Foods recently introduced to the Northern reservations, like chile and canned vegetables, are served along with the traditional meats and soups,

Blackfeet family eating under brush arbor.

fried bread, and the staple of Indian existence, coffee (usually served black with great portions of sugar). Ice-cold tea or lemonade is usually kept handy for the singers and dancers.

In the old days the Indians never knew how much food would be available for the next meal, so they gorged themselves at such feasts. I am still amazed at seeing the great helping (including seconds, thirds, and so on) of food that each individual is capable of consuming. In a poor society, one meal may very well have to suffice for more than one day.

The Indians' dictum has always been: What one cannot eat, one takes home with him. This is considered to be in perfect taste, and a host would be insulted if you did not partake of a proffered meal enthusiastically. As poor as the Indians generally are, food is always shared, even with a stranger, and to refuse an Indian's hospitality is tantamount to plain poor manners on a reservation. It is common to see Indians bringing biscuit tins or freezer jars to a feast for the sole purpose of carrying away what they cannot eat on the spot.

My family and I were once invited to a feast at the Red Cloud community on the Pine Ridge Reservation. The feast, a memorial feast, was held in honor of a deceased son of Alice Red Cloud, one of the fine matriarchs of the community. Although the feast was held primarily as a family affair, nearly 200 distant relatives arrived. Many arrived with different kinds of foods to add to the already overladen table.

Many preparations were taken to insure an abundance of food at the feast. Early in the morning Mrs. Red Cloud's son and son-in-law (the latter an Arapaho, who had made a special trip from his reservation 300 miles away for the occasion) went out hunting for deer and came back late in the morning with two fine specimens. They immediately skinned and butchered them. Other relatives were digging a deep trench, which would serve as the fire pit. One toothless old-timer arrived early with his contribution—a dead mongrel dog— which he unceremoniously swung by the tail and dumped on the woodpile.

In addition to food, many of the arrivals brought fancy embroidered items—pillowcases, sheets, and quilts —which would be given away to those who were especially close to the family or who had helped out with the preparation of the feast.

Just before noon, the guests began to arrive. There were some of the ancient people of the Sioux, men with long braids, old women in long cotton dresses, shawls, and moccasins, their leathery skin bearing more wrinkles than they were years old, and a plethora of Indian children, running and scampering about.

The people began to seat themselves on wooden benches and folding chairs under the shade of a stand of cottonwoods and elms, which was like an oasis on the hot and dusty prairie.

By this time the deermeat and beef were boiling in huge pots on the fire pit. The hair had been singed off the dog, and it was boiling in a separate pot. Two of the men placed tables in the middle of the shaded spot, and the women began to arrange their foods. Meanwhile, the people sat around smoking Bull Durham and store-bought cigarettes and talking about the events in town.

Soon an announcer stood up, welcomed all the people, and briefly told them about the sponsors of the feast and the intention for which it was given. An Indian clergyman, a Protestant minister, rose and read a few passages from the Bible translated into Lakota, the language of the Pine Ridge Sioux. Now it was time to give the Indian blessing.

Two Arapaho, Mrs. Red Cloud's son-in-law and an older man, who was a leading shaman back on the Wind River reservation, performed a short, impressive Indian benediction. They took pieces of *wasna,* the Sioux pemmican, and bits of fried bread, and buried a little of the food at each of the four main compass points. They placed the remaining bits in the center of the shaded area, which represented the center of the Indian universe. By so burying the food, they believed that they were feeding the spirit of the person for whom the memorial feast was being given. After the short ceremony was concluded, the cooks began to distribute the food to the guests at their seats. As in all Sioux functions, the men were seated on one side and the women opposite them.

What an array of food! In addition to the deermeat and beef, there were dishes of chicken, pemmican, and jerky; bowls of boiled potatoes, potato salad, and cole slaw; fried bread, loaves of white bread, and boxes of salted crackers. Just when it seemed that the servers were running out of food, they would return to the table and produce more pots of simmering vegetables, traditional foods such as boiled turnips, soups made from dried chokecherries, buffalo berries, and wild plums. Just when one thought one couldn't swallow another bite, the men served apple, blueberry, and chokecherry pies and chocolate cake—all washed down with thick, syrupy black coffee.

My wife, afraid that she might eat by mistake a tender filet of hound, gave away each morsel of meat served her to an old woman who stood ready with a biscuit tin. She did not know that the dog was served only to the oldest men assembled there.

The Indians gorged themselves—and so did I. The afternoon ended with the dogs fighting over discarded bones, old women packing their biscuit tins to the brim with food to take home, and a severe case of indigestion for one overindulgent white man.

5 The Warrior Nations

O N THE Northern Plains, courage and fortitude were the greatest virtues for a man. The lives of men centered around proving their bravery on the battlefield. War was a way of life.

The young child was raised accordingly. He was taught games by his male relatives which conditioned him for warfare at an early age. Children learned the importance of silence, lest they be detected by an enemy lurking nearby.

But, unlike modern warfare as we know it, the Northern Plains Indians did not fight to conquer an enemy's lands. Of course, there were times when a hostile tribe invaded the hunting domain of another, but the invaders did not think in terms of occupation of another territory. Land was not considered a negotiable commodity. Each tribe had more land than it could use.

No Indian tribe tried to conquer another; one tribe was not interested in ruling another. There was no concept of slavery, as we know it. The Indian did not

Four Claws, a Sioux warrior in full dress carrying a three-bladed war club. Photo by F. B. Fiske.
(Courtesy Plume Trading and Sales Company)

expect others to do his work, hunt his food, or maintain his household.

Why, then, did Indians fight at all? They fought to assert individual bravery and fortitude, for it had been handed down through the ages that the only way to distinguish oneself was to be brave in battle. Only those who could successfully join a war party would be recognized as leaders of their people. Only those who returned to their villages to brag of their exploits could wear badges of honor and be acclaimed by their tribesmen and womenfolk in the honor songs.

Bravery was not necessarily synonymous with killing enemies. Scanning the literature of Northern Plains Indians, we find that the greatest method of gaining recognition on the battlefield was not by killing an enemy, but by touching him with a harmless stick, or bow, and getting away to tell the tale. Was it not greater to approach an armed enemy with no weapon of your own save a stick or an open hand? The Indians thought it was. Naturally, in the course of war there were killings, but they were few compared to the number of adversaries who simply rushed to strike one another. This is known as counting coup, from the French word for strike. The bravest warrior was determined by the number of coups he had counted. Sometimes coups were also counted against his enemy's horses or even his women and children for it was only the fearless warrior who could sneak into his enemy's village to reach the women and children.

While killing or conquering another's land or forcing another tribe into servility were not primary reasons for going into battle, there were other valid reasons.

One of the primary reasons for organizing a war party was to take revenge on an enemy for killing a member of one's family or tribe. The war party might be organized by anyone; it was not mandatory to be a chief. Often it was a brother or father or someone else close to a relative who had been killed in battle. The organizer would call a group of men who knew the deceased and tell them it was time to seek revenge. Then the warriors

Blackfeet warrior with lance and shield.

would prepare by sharpening their weapons and having extra pairs of moccasins made for them if they were to travel a long way on foot. A life for a life was the credo, and it was not considered necessary to go out and kill many enemies unless the revenge was for an entire raiding party that had been wiped out. If the warriors were successful in carrying out their vendetta, the debt was considered paid off.

Often the reason for going against an enemy tribe was to capture horses. In addition to a man being known for his bravery, his status was raised considerably, depending on his wealth. As has been stated before, his wealth was determined largely by the number of possessions he owned. Of all possessions, the most valuable was the horse, for it was the horse that carried the hunter after buffalo and moved his camp from place to place.

Horse stealing played a prominent part in the life of the Plains warrior, but again, it was the risk involved in stealing the horses that counted, as well as the total number of horses stolen. In order to obtain horses from the enemy, it was necessary to sneak into the enemy's camp, exposing oneself to overwhelming odds and certain death if discovered. Thus, it was considered braver to capture one horse picketed near its owner's tipi than it was to run off an entire herd left out to graze away from the village.

Often, men would have a vision that it would be propitious to go on the warpath. They would be given instructions in their dreams of how to organize the war party and successfully attack their enemies. The one who had received such a vision would then assemble a group of warriors and tell them about his vision. The Indians were known to have preferred a surprise attack and most of the time would retreat from a pitched battle against superior numbers. Sometimes the leader of a war party would have another vision before he and his men reached their enemy's camp. If the vision told him that the war party was going to be unsuccessful, they would return home immediately.

Among the Sioux, the organizer of the war party to capture one horse picketed near its owner's tipi than night and serve them a buffalo feast. He would then relate his vision, saying that he had been instructed to make up a war party to attack the Shoshoni or Utes. He would appoint several men *blokaunta*, a sort of lieutenant, each of whom were in charge of three or four men. It would be the duty of the *blokaunta* to make sure his men did not attack the enemy before a general signal was given. Should they attack prematurely, they might reveal the whereabouts of the entire war party, which could lead to mass destruction.

Once the signal had been given, it was every man for himself. There was usually no general plan of attack. Each man singled out an opponent and fought hand to hand. There was great honor in being the first to strike the enemy. Among the Crow and Sioux, four men might count coup on the same enemy, but the greatest honor went to the men who struck first. Often, during the thick of battle, a warrior might call attention to his individual deeds by exclaiming in a loud voice, "I, Running Horse, count first coup on the enemy" as he hit his opponent with a coupstick, or bow. Often, the counting of the first coup was disputed by two men. Later they settled their dispute by taking a vow that if they lied, they would be killed within the year.

With such emphasis on warfare as a part of daily life, it is only fitting that there should have been an abundance of organizations that specialized in warfare among

the Indian tribes of the Northern Plains. Military societies or organizations of prominent warriors were very
popular. A warrior who became noteworthy for his
battle record achieved further distinction by joining one
of many war societies. Often, there were societies for
young boys modeled after their fathers' clubs.

The military societies differed in structure and function, depending on each tribe, but basically they had
their own emblems, songs, dances, and ritualistic paraphernalia. Most of the societies were founded by men
who had dreamed of starting such an organization and
received their instructions from supernatural beings in
their visions.

The military, or soldier, societies differed from other
associations, inasmuch as their sole function was war.
The societies often vied with one another within the
same tribe for prominent members and recognition.

One of the best-known soldier societies was the Dog
Soldiers, a Cheyenne fraternity of warriors. To the Dog
Soldiers fell the special responsibility of policing the
camp, punishing offenders of civil law, and acting as
guards on tribal hunts.

Sometimes, the soldier societies went on the warpath
as a group. One of the most spectacular of societies
was the Sioux Strong Hearts. Some members wore a
long otter skin sash which trailed over one shoulder to
the ground. They were lauded as the bravest of all Sioux
warriors. During the thick of battle, the sash wearer
staked the end of his sash to the ground, thus declaring
that he would not retreat from the spot. No matter how
hot the battle was, the sash wearer could not remove the
stake. If the entire society decided that the odds were
against it and that it must retreat, another member of

the society had to run up to the sash wearer and remove the stake, thus releasing him. If the sash wearer removed the stake himself while under fire from the enemy and escaped, he was forever ridiculed by the other members. Assuming the role of sash wearer was voluntary, but once pledged, the warrior had to suffer the consequences.

Among the Crow were two prominent societies, the Foxes and the Lumpwoods. The former took its name from its founder, who had received a vision of many foxes. The Lumpwoods took their name from their society emblem, which was a four-foot club made of knotty wood. These two societies epitomized the rivalry between military societies, for it was common for them to go on expeditions for the sole purpose of stealing each others' wives! If a wife was stolen, it was the law of Crow society that she should remain with her captor, and the former husband could be punished if he tried to recapture her.

The names of the societies differed from tribe to tribe, some having such strange names as the Mandan Half-Shaved Heads or the Blackfeet Mosquitoes, but all shared the fact that they had their own songs, costumes, dances, and paraphernalia. Some members were elected officials and had the right to carry the emblems of the society—spears, drums, headdresses—and each society had its own rules, which the members were forced to follow even to their deaths.

Some of the tribes had societies which were graded, most notably the Blackfeet (including the Piegan and Blood), Gros Ventre, Arapaho, Mandan, and Hidatsa, and boys moved from one society to another, depending on their ages. The potential member also had to purchase the right to join. In other tribes, however, the boy could join any society he chose. While he was free to move from one society to another, he usually stayed with the society to which he first pledged allegiance.

The Indian boy went on his first warpath when he was twelve to fourteen years of age. By this time he had been taught how to use a bow and arrow by his uncle, father, or other male relative. The Indian boy was constantly reminded by his family that unless he could provide food for his people or be courageous on the battlefield, he could never expect to take his place among the rest of the warriors of the village.

It was a great honor for a boy to be asked to accompany men on the warpath for the first time. He knew that on the first warpath the other men would try to test his courage. One such method of testing was called the water carrier's ordeal.

Late some night, when the war party had stopped to camp, the boy was given a buffalo paunch and told to go find water and bring it back to the men. The boy was given no directions, but he had to find a creek by himself in the darkness. Traveling alone at night was enough of an ordeal, but after finding water, the boy had to be careful not to spill the water from the paunch as he returned to the camp. His courage would be measured by the amount of water in the paunch. If the paunch was not full, it indicated that he was afraid and had spilled the water in his haste to return to the camp.

The men customarily played jokes on the novice warrior as part of the initiation. Sometimes the paunch was given to the boy, and he was told to fill it with water and deliver it to a certain man in the war party. Upon returning, the boy would seek out the man, but when found, the man stated that he wanted no water, and designated another man to whom the boy should deliver it. Again the boy would seek out another man, and again he would be told there was a mistake, being directed to still another. This continued until the boy made the circuit of the camp, only to find out at the end that the men were playing a joke on him.

Thus, the Indian boy accompanied his elders on the warpath, doing chores for them, cooking, carrying the packs of extra moccasins and meat for the journey. On his first time out, he might not be required actually to attack an enemy or steal a horse, but he would learn the responsibilities of a warrior. Soon the time would come when he could discard his childhood name and take one more appropriate for a warrior.

The naming of a child was an important occasion among all the tribes—one highlighted with the giving of gifts by the parents, feasting by the entire village, and all-night dancing to the songs honoring the newly named. The first naming took place shortly after birth. An old man or woman with a reputation for being wise was called in by the parents to confer an appropriate name on the newborn. The name usually commemorated an event that occurred in the village during the time of the baby's birth.

It is said about a famous Oglala Sioux chief that when he was born, a strange formation of crimson clouds appeared in the Western skies. A sacred woman of the tribe came to the lodge of the newborn and told the parents of the wonderful sight and honored the baby with the name Red Cloud. As soon as the child was named, a herald proclaimed the news throughout the village, telling the people to prepare for a great feast, because a new warrior had been born. A buffalo was cooked, and the men and women put on their best clothing for the dance to follow. It was a time for great merriment in the camp.

After a child grew older and proved himself on the warpath, his childhood name was discarded, and he was given a new one. This time the name might be handed down from a noble warrior who had died, or a new name describing a brave feat in combat might be given to him.

There was once a Hunkpapa Sioux boy named Slow. He was an awkward boy who deliberated at great length before he spoke. He was slow at games, even at eating. He could not run or swim very fast. A more fitting name could not have been given him. But when he reached the age of fourteen, he went out on his first war party. During a battle, Slow faced an armed enemy, he himself weaponless except for a coupstick. The enemy was about to let an arrow fly when all of a sudden Slow struck with incredible speed. He knocked down the enemy warrior with a quick thrust of his coupstick and cried out, "I, Slow, have struck the enemy." His comrades looked on in amazement while his father, who also had accompanied the war party, beamed with pride.

When Slow returned to the village, there was a victory dance. Slow's father paraded his son around the camp on a new horse and announced that on this day his brave son's childhood name would be "thrown away" and a more appropriate name given to the fledgling warrior. The once-awkward boy's new name was to become known to all the Indians and white men on the Northern Plains. He was called Sitting Bull.

Before the white man arrived with guns and ammunition, the Northern Plains Indians relied on only a few types of weapons, such as bows and arrows; lances; war clubs, or tomahawks; knives; and shields. After the white man arrived on the Plains, his guns and ammunition, as well as metal arrow points, knives, hatchets, and sabers, were in great demand.

If an Indian tribe won a victory over a group of soldiers, it was careful to strip the soldiers of all their valuable possessions. For it was difficult to obtain large amounts of ammunition, even though firearms were readily available at most of the trading posts and forts before the major wars between the Indians and the United States Government began on the Plains.

Bows were usually small, four or five feet in length, with a string made of twisted sinew. Small bows were especially effective when used by a mounted warrior, since a longer bow only hampered him. A good horseman could attack his enemy riding at full speed and drop down under the horse's neck, from which vantage point he could shoot his arrows, with his mount serving as a shield for his body.

Arrows were originally made with flint arrowheads, but these were later replaced with metal points obtained from the traders or fashioned from tin cans. Either two or three feathers were used on the arrow to guide its flight. It is said that an arrow with three feathers flew straighter but that one with two feathers was faster.

Lances and spears were usually about 6 feet in length and had a stone or metal point. Some were elaborately decorated with feathers and fur and served as emblems of various warrior societies. Spears were very rarely thrown, but usually thrust at an enemy. Some

An Arapaho woman named Powder Face carrying a crooked lance, metal tomahawk, and wearing a warbonnet. Indian women usually carried the weapons of their relatives in the Victory dances. This photo was taken by William S. Soule between 1867 and 1874.

warriors carried a rawhide shield made from the heavy hump of a buffalo hide. The shield not only could effectively deflect arrows, but was known to occasionally turn aside a bullet. When not in use, it was sometimes kept in a decorated covering or placed outside the tipi on a special tripod, along with other weapons, where it was ready in case of a sudden attack.

War clubs were very effective, in either fighting on foot or on horseback. Before metal hatchets were introduced by the traders, most war clubs were made by attaching an oval rock to a wooden handle, which was wrapped with wet rawhide to give it durability. Some clubs were made so that the head was attached solidly to the handle, while others were made so that the head was suspended from the handle by a few inches of braided or twisted rawhide, giving it a mace and chain effect. There was usually a buckskin or rawhide loop at the end of the handle of the war club, which the warrior could easily slip over his hand and hold until ready to use. A war club was a dangerous weapon and, with maximum force, could smash the head of an opponent. One of the most gruesome war clubs was made from the stock of a rifle, into which two or three knife blades were inserted.

Although the rifle was a deadly innovation in the techniques of Plains Indian warfare, its use was rather limited. Even in the last of the Indian wars, the primary fighting tools were the ancient bows and arrows, lances, and clubs. Ammunition was never in abundance, and target shooting was unheard of, because the Indian warriors didn't want to waste what little ammunition they had. The only time Indians fired their weapons was on the battlefield, so they were generally bad shots. The weapon was effective at close range, but long-distance shooting was ineffective. While rifles were carried in elaborately fringed and beaded cases slung over their shoulders or saddles, Indians usually neglected to care for their weapons like the United States soldier did. It was many years before the Indians learned how to clean a rifle. Cleaning rods were usually discarded as non-essential equipment.

A warrior fighting on horseback usually held his arrows in his teeth for easy access. Shields were slipped over the left arm, and the knife was carried in a rawhide scabbard. Some wore bone breastplates, which hung from neck to waist for additional protection against arrows. A war club was held in the right hand for close fighting where a warrior could swoop down on an enemy and easily strike a fatal blow.

Usually the warriors carried little extra clothing or paraphernalia that might hamper them in fighting or slow down their traveling. They usually stripped down to a breechcloth and moccasins before the fight. Some would wear various insignia or charms that assured their good fortune in battle. Such charms—the skin of an animal or bird, a tuft of buffalo hair, or the claws of a bear or eagle—would be worn around their necks or carried in a small bag from their belts. Warrior societies might carry the emblems of their lodges, which often included a long-stemmed pipe. Among the Sioux, one such warrior society carried a filled pipe sealed with the fat of a buffalo. If the warriors were successful, the leader unsealed the pipe, and all the warriors smoked.

The actual battle gave each warrior the opportunity

to prove his ability and win the honors of the day. One of the bravest feats was to rescue a warrior who had been dismounted in battle. A comrade would suddenly dash to his aid and pick him up on the back of his own horse. This was considered an act of heroism second to none, for often the dismounted warrior drew the attention of all the enemy warriors eager to rush him and count coup.

Scalping and mutilation of bodies has been widely reported in early literature, as well as in movies and on television. According to some writers today, it would appear that every Indian was out to acquire as many scalps as he could. It is questionable, however, that scalping was a widespread practice. A warrior in the thick of battle hardly had time to scalp a fallen foe without exposing himself to great risk. True, the scalp became a trophy, proof that the warrior had killed a foe, but scalps could be taken only if an entire enemy force had been annihilated and there was leisure time to actually do the scalping.

That scalping was indigenous to the Northern Plains is also questionable. Many scholars believe that the practice was originally conceived by white men living in the East, who paid their Indian allies bounty for the scalps of their enemies. However initiated, scalping was practiced by all the Northern Plains tribes until they were put on reservations. Most Indians, if asked today, would say that they (not the white man) had originated the practice.

After scalping had come into vogue on the Plains, many myths sprang up around it. Some believed, for instance, that if an enemy was not scalped, his spirit would be waiting for its slayer in the Spirit World, where

Mutilation of enemies was practiced on the Northern Plains. Here is a drawing by W. H. Gill in 1907 of a Cheyenne necklace made from fingers of Indians killed by the Cheyenne, High Wolf.

it would take revenge. The taking of the scalp therefore deprived an enemy of his soul and later allowed the slayer to slip into the hereafter with no fear of reprisal.

Scalps that were brought back to the village were usually stretched on frames and hung from poles. These poles were carried by the female relatives of the warriors in the victory dance. This was an occasion for everyone in the village to dress in his best clothing and join in the singing and the dancing. During the celebration the warriors would stand up individually in the center of the gathering and recount their deeds, acting out their heroic conquests in pantomime and sign language while the singers sang bold praises of their accomplishments. A warrior would begin his harangue by striking a pole with his war club or coupstick, signifying his striking of an enemy, and proceed to tell the gathering how he had overpowered his opponent. When he finished his soliloquy, the audience would respond with utterances of approval while the singers struck the drum in applause.

After public recital of his war record, a warrior was generally qualified to wear a feather for each enemy slain or coup counted. If an enemy had been killed, a feather might be painted red; if his throat had been cut, a warrior might cut a notch in the feather. Among the Sioux, a warrior who had counted the first coup was entitled to wear a single eagle feather sticking upright behind his head. The one to count the second coup wore his feather diagonally to the right behind his head. The third coup entitled the warrior to wear his feather diagonally to the left; the fourth, to wear it hanging downward.

If a man had collected a number of coup feathers, he was entitled to wear a warbonnet, the most well-known headdress of the Plains. Each feather signified a battle deed, so it was only the bravest of warriors who could wear such a headdress. Some of the headdresses trailed to the ground, and those who wore them could immediately be identified as men who had made many forays against the enemy. Among some tribes, the wives and sisters of brave warriors wore their husbands' warbonnets in the victory dance.

If a man had collected a number of scalps, he might tie them to his lodge poles as fair warning to any enemy who came too close to his village. His outstanding battle records were often painted in pictographs on his tipi cover. Scalps were also used to decorate "hair shirts," which were worn at public functions.

When the Northern Plains Indians were placed on reservations in the latter part of the nineteenth century, their freedom to seek out their enemies was greatly inhibited. War did not end, however, and Indians still found it possible to slip off the reservation for a quick attack on a hostile tribe not too far away. The old methods of war did not end until after the Indian wars of the 1860's and 1870's against the United States. The last official battle between the Indians and whites took place on Wounded Knee Creek on the Pine Ridge Indian Reservation between a band of Sioux and the United States Cavalry. This was known as the Wounded Knee Massacre, in which a small ragged group of Sioux were brutally slaughtered by United States forces. The date was December 29, 1890, a day in which all hostilities between the United States and the Indians came to a halt. Ironically, twenty-seven years later, thousands of American Indians volunteered to serve with the United States forces in World War I. Indian and white animosities seemed to be overshadowed by the common threat to the United States, and soon Indian and white soldiers fought side by side against Germany and her allies. The gallantry of the Indian soldier prompted Congress to confer equal citizenship upon all American Indians on June 2, 1924. Up to that time only about two-thirds of the Indians had enjoyed citizenship through treaty rights.

Participation in World War I had a great effect upon the reservation Indians. The old victory songs and

(Smithsonian Institution)

Sioux women at Grand River, South Dakota, performing the Round dance, a vestige of the old Victory dance. The second, third, and fourth women from the right wear trade cloth dresses decorated with dentalium shells. The first, fourth, and fifth women have dresses decorated with cowry shells. Photo by Frances Densmore around 1900.

dances were reinstated, only now the people sang of the Indian boys who had gone "over there" and fought against the enemies of the United States. Soldiers returning from the war were treated just like the warriors of old who returned from the warpath. They were feasted, and special songs were sung in their honor. The soldiers, dressed in sharp military dress instead of the feathered costumes of old, attended great celebrations in their honor and spoke of their valorous deeds against the Germans. As in the old days, the people responded with *hau*'s and the singers hit the drum in applause. The female relatives of the soldiers danced in the victory

A Victory dance held for a returning soldier on the Pine Ridge Indian Reservation, September 14, 1945. Indians have volunteered for active duty in the Armed Forces since World War I.

dances; but instead of carrying scalps, they carried captured German flags and other souvenirs picked up on the battlefields of a distant land.

When World War II was declared, Indians again volunteered for active duty. New songs were composed in honor of the returning heroes, telling about the fall of Berlin and the bombing of Tokyo. Despite their ruthless treatment by the United States Government in the previous century and their placement on reservations, the Indians became super-patriots of the land. Their patriotism and valor has been consistent through the Korean conflict and Vietnam. Officers today still tell of their bravery in battle, and many have been awarded the

Congressional Medal of Honor. There is a noticeable absence of Indian draftees; most of them volunteer.

Today, Indian military service is further attested to by the prevalence of American Legion posts and Veterans of Foreign Wars organizations on reservations. These organizations often sponsor Indian celebrations, and their members show up wearing their old uniforms. Although in some ways the Indian celebrations are similar to those held long ago, most begin with an Indian "national anthem," a patriotic song sung in the native dialect, which accompanies the raising of the American flag and a three-gun salute. There is a strange beauty in it. Around the camp circle sit the ancient Indians, smoking their long-stemmed pipes and conversing in their native Indian language, when suddenly a uniformed color guard of soldiers enters the dance area with the American flag. At the raising of the flag and the firing of a salute, the children rush in to pick up the empty cartridges ejected by the riflemen. Soon the singers begin a war song in the ancient, vocally tense method of Indian singing.

The way the Indian feels about the land he lives on and his sense of responsibility to the United States Government are best summed up in one national anthem composed by the Sioux at Pine Ridge. Before each celebration, a group of singers start with the song:

The flag of the United States will fly forever
Underneath it, the Indian people will grow

6 The Spirit Path

MANY of the Plains tribes believed that before living on earth, they had dwelled in subterranean caverns in total darkness. One day, their legends say, one of their tribe saw something wonderful, a pinpoint of light streaming into the cave. He followed the ray to its source and discovered, to his amazement, daylight and the surface of the earth. He immediately returned to his people and led them out of darkness into the new world.

Upon moving onto the earth, the tribe's culture hero, a mythological man with magical powers who sometimes played pranks on the people, taught them how to build their dwellings, hunt buffalo, make their clothing, and all the things that were necessary to live. And so the Indians were born to the world.

Many of the Indian myths are like old Greek and Roman myths. The Sun and Moon are personified; they marry and have children, fight against lesser gods for power, and seek the worship of mankind on earth. All the gods in the stories have names, and in the olden days the tribal storytellers were able to relate the lives of the supernatural and lay the foundation for the everyday religious beliefs of the people.

In a society devoid of science and technology, even the simplest manifestations of nature are worthy of praise and adoration. What caused day and night, the sun to burn in the sky, the moon to change its form during the month? What made the seasons change, the snow fall, and the wind blow in the trees? These questions, unanswerable to the inquisitive Indian mind in common terms, provided the basis for his belief in nature and the supernatural. The forces that caused nature to unfold before the Indians' eyes were given names, and ceremonies were conducted to ask for help, strength, and power. The rock, the tree, the wind, the water, all were manifestations of a spiritual force.

Whether or not the Indian believed in a supreme god before white missionaries arrived is difficult to prove today. Some authorities believe that the Indian probably called on a host of gods, each of whom specialized in certain kinds of assistance. A man going to war, for instance, might pray to a certain deity to give him strength and cunning on the warpath, while another man prayed to a different divinity to give him good luck in hunting. Other scholars say that while the Indian believed in many gods, or spiritual forces, there was always one supreme god, who in essence ruled over the other lesser gods. The missionaries used this concept to teach Indians about the Christian concept of God. Today, most Indians believe that they orignally worshipped one god, but it is apparent that their thinking has been influenced greatly by many years of Christian teaching.

In ancient times the average Indian spent a great deal of time propitiating his gods through prayer, self-sacrifice, pilgrimages, and formal ceremonies. While many of the elements of Plains worship were similar,

Little Chief, an Assiniboine shaman, praying before a tree to be used as the sacred pole in a Sun dance. Photo taken by Sumner W. Matteson at the Fort Belknap Reservation, Montana, in July, 1906.

such as the vision quest, the Sun dance, Sweat Lodge, and various ceremonies related to birth, death, and initiation to adult life, each tribe had its own individual way of conducting these ceremonies. There was also a great deal of variation in ceremonies within one tribe.

The key figure in formal ceremonies was the religious leader, often referred to as the medicine man or shaman. The terms are not always interchangeable, for a medicine man usually dealt with herbs and was called upon to heal the wounded and cure the sick through the use of medicines made from roots, leaves, grasses, and other natural elements. A shaman, on the other hand, while he might use some herbs in his treatment of the sick, usually relied on supernatural power. He was often a conjurer, or magician, who was capable of amazing his followers with his mystical abilities. He might, for instance, diagnose the cause of pain as the result of a demon possessing the afflicted person. With a modicum of sleight of hand, he could suck out the source of the patient's illness through a bone tube, spitting out a bird or rock or other substance, which had allegedly caused the illness. Each shaman was a well-known member of the tribal community and was often paid very well in horses and robes for treating his patients. Part of his popularity was based on his method of conducting curing ceremonies, so it is logical that many ceremonies in one tribe varied between one practitioner and another. In many cases, the popular shaman was the one who could put on the best show.

In addition to curing, the shaman was also called on for consultation in matters of war, hunting, moving camp, naming children, and analyzing dreams and visions. In formal ceremonies, such as the Sun dance, he served as an intermediary between the spirits and the men who performed the ritual; some served as directors of the dance. Because of their supernatural abilities, they were often feared by the common people, who believed they were capable of witchcraft and black magic.

Perhaps there is nothing more universal in all Plains religion than the use of the long-stemmed pipe, often called the peace pipe but, more correctly, the sacred pipe. The pipe was essentially a medium of prayer. When a man prayed with a pipe, the smoke rose and carried his message upward to a particular god. Pipe smoking was a necessary prelude to every religious ceremony and was also done by individuals before

(Smithsonian Institution) Nosey, also known as Yellow Lodge, was an Assiniboine who served as leader of the Sun dance in 1905. This photo was taken by Sumner Matteson, July 6, 1905, in the shaman's tipi.

leaving on the hunt or warpath. Usually each man owned his own pipe and carried it in an elaborately decorated pipe bag.

The prized pipe was, and still is, one made with a catlinite bowl. Catlinite is a red stone that is found only in the pipestone quarry near Pipestone, Minnesota. The bowl was made separately from the pipestem, and it was considered unlucky among some tribes to keep the bowl attached to the stem when the pipe was stored. Because the pipe was powerful in carrying prayers to the gods, it was treated with a great deal of respect by all people. Children were not allowed to touch the pipe or even approach it, for fear that they would pick it up and play with it. Such an action could cause a great disaster, even death, to someone in the offender's family.

Because tobacco was smoked in the pipe, it, too, had

certain sacred powers, and was often used independently, as an offering to the spirits. There were various kinds of tobacco developed by the Indians, in addition to the tobacco plant, which was cultivated by such tribes as the Crow and those living in permanent villages on the Missouri River. Tobacco was often made from the inner bark of the red willow and from certain dried leaves. Often, this "Indian tobacco" was mixed with roots to give it a special aroma. Today, while commercial tobacco is readily available on the reservations, the older Indians still prefer to make their own. However, among the store-bought variety, Bull Durham is still in great demand. Not only do the Indians like to roll their own cigarettes; the packages of loose tobacco are used ceremonially, as offerings. When the tobacco is used up, the Bull Durham sacks are often filled with cotton or grass and tied to sticks as drumbeaters.

Among the Crow, tobacco was considered so important to the general welfare of the tribe that they instituted a tobacco society, whose members were given the task of seeing to the planting and harvesting of the tobacco crops. Both men and women belonged, and they had their own songs and dances and ceremonies, most of which were of a secret nature. To the Crow, tobacco was synonymous with medicine, and they believed that it was bestowed upon their tribe by supernatural sources.

The Plains tribes believed in a hereafter, a place where the spirits went to live after death. As in many early societies, it was believed that a man lived in a place similar to earth, where there were plenty of buffalo to hunt and always food for the people. When a man died, his personal possessions—his clothing, wea-

This photograph of an unusual burial was taken by A. B. Coe at Piegan, Montana. It is probably Blackfeet.

pons, and favorite horse—were buried with him so that they might be of service to him in the other world. Likewise, a women was buried with her best cooking and sewing utensils.

Forms of burial varied, but the most common on the Plains was the scaffold, or tree, burial. The deceased was dressed in his finest clothing and wrapped in a buffalo hide. Then the body was placed in a tree or on a scaffold, where it remained until it decomposed. Indians were generally fearful that a person's spirit haunted the place of its burial, so such places were usually avoided. Sometimes relatives might come near the burial grounds to mourn for their loved ones. They would often gash their bodies or cut their hair short and blacken their faces with paint to show their grief. It was also customary for the close relatives of the deceased to give away all their possessions after someone had died.

The Sioux mourned their dead for one year. There was a special ceremony called Keeping the Ghost, in which a close relative would keep a lock of the deceased's hair in a special bundle for one year. Each day the spirit of the deceased was fed by the keeper, and elaborate ceremonies were held in its behalf. At the end of one year, the spirit was formally freed and the spirit keeping ceremony fulfilled. Even today the Sioux believe that the spirit of the deceased stays around its home for one year after the person dies, and many of the people set a special plate for the spirit and feed it at each meal. They say that this is an important task, for if the mourner should forget to feed the spirit, it will become angry and might cause harm to its family.

The Sioux also believed that when a person died, the spirit would soon return to summon someone it loved dearly to accompany it to the hereafter. Many of the old people still say that when they hear a baby crying outside in the night or hear a rooster crow in the darkness, it is some boundless spirit calling someone to die. When this occurs, a shaman is called in to burn incense, which will chase the ghost away.

Belief in ghosts was, and still is, common to the Indians of the Northern Plains. Ghosts were capable of advising humans in matters pertaining to the welfare of the tribe. Some men, notably shamans, were capable of communing with ghosts. It is believed that these shamans met ghosts at night and walked and talked with them without fear. The shamans freely asked the advice of ghosts about how to cure people, and the ghosts predicted certain events in the lives of people. They were capable of finding lost articles or things that had been stolen and in some cases were even able to take another life.

One of the best examples of calling upon ghosts for supernatural aid is found in the Yuwipi religion of the Sioux of South Dakota, notably the Oglala and Sicangu living at Pine Ridge and Rosebud.

For a number of years I was fascinated by the stories I heard from the Indian people about the mysterious ceremonies held in darkened houses for the purposes of summoning ghosts to assist in the treatment of the sick and finding lost or stolen articles. In 1966 and 1967 I received grants from the American Philosophical Society to investigate this modern day native religion called Yuwipi. Although I had spent many summers with the Sioux at Pine Ridge studying their music, dance, and language, Yuwipi still remained a mystery to me.

I searched the literature to find any documentation of Yuwipi, but there was very little reported. It was only recently that some anthropologists took an active interest in Yuwipi, and very little had been published. I had heard stories in the past which told of strange noises and sights that were evidenced at these meetings, that certain men had the ability to talk to spirits and learn from them methods of curing the sick. I had also heard stories about what happened to people who went to the Yuwipi meetings and refused to believe in the power of the shamans. Some of the old-timers said that strange creatures would enter the room and remove the disbelievers by throwing them out the window. The Yuwipi men, so the old-timers said, also had the ability to know who among the congregation did not believe and would call them by name and ask them to believe. Faith, it would seem, was just as important in Yuwipi meetings as in formal white man's religions, for the nonbeliever often caused the meetings to be ineffectual. If a nonbeliever was present, the spirits would refuse to come.

And so it was in the summer of 1966 that George Plenty Wolf, a well-known Yuwipi man in the Red Cloud community of Pine Ridge, saw me one day. Knowing my interest in the religion of his people, he informed me of a forthcoming meeting. "Spirit meeting tonight," he said in broken English. "You come."

I was elated on receiving the invitation, and at dusk, the traditional starting time of Yuwipi meetings, I arrived at his daughter's house, where the meeting was to be held. Several people had arrived and were sitting outside the house smoking and talking about the current events of the reservation. Some of the men were busy removing all the furniture from the house. This was important, for the spirits would not come if there were traces of modern, white man's conveniences. After removing the furniture, the men covered the outsides of the windows with tar paper, and the insides with blankets. The room had to be made absolutely dark, for again, the spirits would come only in total darkness. The men placed mattresses and blankets around the perimeter of the room for the people to sit on. Just as the sun sank and darkness was imminent, the people began to enter the room.

Plenty Wolf arrived with his son Basil, who was to act as his assistant, and his wife Julie, who also "helped him pray." Although the room was small, there were more than thirty people crammed in against the walls. Near the door sat two men with hand drums, who were to provide the all-important singing for the meeting.

Plenty Wolf and his son began to arrange the sacred altar in the center of the floor. Plenty Wolf placed a suitcase filled with religious paraphernalia on the floor beside him and opened it. It contained a pipe and pipe bag, two gourd rattles, several willow sticks, some sacks of Bull Durham, and miscellaneous feathers and medicines, which were part of his sacred altar.

His son stepped outside and soon returned with seven coffee cans filled with dirt. He set them around the room at the corners of the sacred place. He also spread sage on the inside of the altar. Into the coffee cans he inserted the willow sticks to which were tied different colored offerings of cloth: black for the west, red for the north, yellow for the east, and white for the south. He also tied on a blue cloth to represent the sky and a green one for the earth. In the center of the altar, between the blue and green flags, was a seventh can, which contained Plenty Wolf's personal *tunkan,* or sacred stone, neatly kept in a small beaded pouch suspended from a forked willow branch.

To put the final touches on the altar, Basil unrolled a string containing several hundred small cloth bundles of tobacco in such a way that the *canli wapahte,* as it is called, formed an outline around the altar. Then Plenty Wolf spread earth collected from a mole's burrow in the altar and smoothed it with the face of a hand drum. Around it he placed a shorter string of thirty-two bundles of tobacco. The altar being completed, Basil handed out to each one of the devotees a sprig of sage, which each one placed over his ear. Followers of Yuwipi believe that the spirits will recognize anyone who wears the sage as a true believer. The tobacco contained in the bundles was an individual offering to the hundreds of spirits who were going to visit the meeting place that night.

Since total darkness was a prerequisite of the meeting, Plenty Wolf called for the single light that burned in the room to be turned out momentarily so he could determine whether the room was dark enough. Satisfied with the blackness of the room, he called for the light to be turned on again and began to fill the sacred pipe.

He took the Indian tobacco from his pouch and ceremonially placed seven pinches of tobacco into the pipe bowl, one for each compass point, the earth, and the sky, and the seventh for the Spotted Eagle, which was the messenger of the great Spirit.

As he filled the pipe, the singers began in loud, clear voices:

> Friend, say this and fill the pipe
> Say, "I want to live with all my relatives"
> If you do, it will be so

The significance of this song is found in one underlying philosophy of the Yuwipi religion—the welfare of the whole tribe.

Plenty Wolf then stuffed a sprig of sage into the pipe bowl and handed it to his wife. *"Yusni yo,"* he said upon conclusion. "Turn out the lights."

There was instant darkness. Plenty Wolf began to pray in Sioux while the singers sang appropriate music in loud voices. Plenty Wolf told of the vision which had given him the power to conduct these meetings. Once he had gone to a lonely place high on a hilltop. There he prayed for two days, and soon thereafter he received a vision from the Great Spirit instructing him in the rituals he was conducting tonight. His power went unquestioned by the people, for it was said that he had the ability to cure the sick even when the white man's doctors had failed. Everyone was silent except for an occasional cough by a devotee or fearful sob by a small child.

When he had finished the prayer and the singers had concluded their song, Plenty Wolf asked for the light to be turned on again.

He then handed the pipe to his wife for her to hold during the next part of the ceremony. He summoned his son and the lead singer to get a quilt and rawhide rope, which was hanging on a nail next to the door. First they bound his hands together behind his back. The two men took the quilt and placed it over Plenty Wolf's head and body so that all but his feet were completely covered with it. Then they took the rawhide rope, one end of which had been fashioned into a noose, and slipped it over the blanketed outline of his head. They quickly wrapped the rope around him, tying it in an overhand knot behind his body, and secured it tightly around his ankles.

His muffled voice through the blanket told them that the rope had been secured well. The two men then picked up the Yuwipi man and laid him facedown on a bed of sage in the center of the altar. Again Plenty Wolf's muffled voice told them to extinguish the light. It was now time for the spirits to enter the meeting place.

The singers once again started, but now all the people who knew the song joined in. The singers had no mercy for the drums; they beat them as loudly as possible, shouting shrilly their supplications to the Great Spirit. The loudness of their voices seemed to be further magnified in the blackness of the small room. Suddenly there was a gigantic crash and thumping on the floor of the cabin. The gourd rattles which had been placed on the altar began to resound in tempo with the frenetic singing. The rattles seemed to come from everywhere—the ceiling, the floor, the walls, over our very heads. The rattles shook erratically, then seemed to pound against the floor in time with the throbbing drums. And then, before my eyes, I began to see blue sparks emit from each place the rattles struck. Now slowly, now quickly, the rattles beat against the small room, sending off their mysterious blue sparks. The spirits had arrived!

The cacaphony of the singing and rattling abruptly subsided, and then there was silence, interrupted occasionally by the soft rattling of the gourds, as if they were talking in a rattle-jargon to the Yuwipi man. They seemed to be, for each time they rattled, he answered them in muffled tones, as if they were talking to him, but one could hear only his response. The time had come for the devotees who so desired to make evident their intentions for attending the meeting. Some were sick. Openly, in the presence of the rest of the people, they told about their illnesses. They asked for assistance for loved ones who were in the armed forces or others who lay in the hospital nearby, afflicted with some disease. It was then that it became apparent to me that the people were not talking to the Yuwipi man, but rather through him, to the spirits present there. As each man and woman ended his plea for help, the Yuwipi man responded with the traditional *hau*, and the rattles likewise answered with barely audible shaking sounds. Those who suffered from slight sicknesses were then commanded to stand up, take hold of the offering flag nearest them, and be cured.

A man sitting next to me asked me if I was sick. I said, "Not really, but I have been plagued with a slight headache tonight." He told me to stand up and grab the flag nearest me. The spirits would take care of the headache. Somewhat reluctantly I fumbled in the darkness and reached out for the flag nearest me. I then stood up. The singers began:

> Stand up, he (the spirit) will look at you
> Grandfather will look at you
> Stand up, he will look at you
> The Buffalo will look at you

Once again the rattles began their resonant dancing on the floors and walls. I stood there not knowing what to expect, apprehensive of the sounds—or rather what produced the sounds—around me. As I stood there, my back to the sacred altar, I suddenly felt the lightest of touches—one on each side of the back of my head. The *thing,* whatever it was, proceeded to caress my head ever so softly, then dropped to my shoulders and up and down my spine. The thing made its way back up to my head, then, as suddenly as it had approached me, disappeared. The singing stopped, and the man sitting next to me grabbed my hand and led me back to my seat.

Then there followed a series of very lively songs, and again the rattles danced hard against the floor, blue sparks popping all around the room. The song instructed anyone who wished to get up and dance in place:

Come dancing and look at them (the spirits)
The four winds are coming to dance flying
Come dancing and look at them

Plenty Wolf, after the song had ended, told the people who had spoken earlier how to cure their sicknesses. He told those who inquired about their loved ones sick in the hospitals how they were faring and asked those of us who had been "cured" on the spot if our illnesses still bothered us. Those who were cured promised to hold a special thanksgiving meeting for the spirits. This was more or less mandatory, for if someone were to have his prayers answered and not offer the prescribed thanksgiving rite, harm might befall him or his family.

Then a special song was sung, during which time the spirits departed and went back to their homes somewhere in the West. The lights were turned on and Plenty Wolf was sitting in the middle of the altar, completely free of his blanket and bindings. The blanket had been flung across the room, landing on the lap of a devotee, while the rope which had bound him was rolled up neatly into a ball next to him. The rolling into a ball is called *yuwipi* in Sioux; hence, the name of the religion.

The sacred pipe, which had remained in the possession of Mrs. Plenty Wolf during the ceremony, was then lighted and passed clockwise around the room to each of the devotees. Each one, man and woman, took the pipe and took a few puffs of it, saying, *"Mitakuye oyasin,"* which translated means "all my relations," once again reaffirming the philosophy that the ceremony was conducted for all the relatives, or people of the tribe. After the pipe smoking, a bowl of water was passed around to all the participants, and each one drank, exclaiming, *"Mitakuye oyasin."* When the ceremonial water drinking was concluded, it was time for the feast, a traditional epilogue to every Yuwipi meeting.

After the meeting, I asked Plenty Wolf what caused the rattling and the sparks.

"The spirits," he answered.

"And how did you get untied?"

Again he replied, "The spirits."

I didn't have to ask what I felt touching me lightly on the head and back. I was sure the credit would have gone to the spirits, who had by now returned to their home in the West.

As for my headache, it had gone away as mysteriously as the spirits!

Just what does cause the mysterious things to happen in the Yuwipi meeting is a matter of conjecture. For the faithful, it is unquestionably the spirit people; for the nonbeliever, the events are usually attributed to sleight of hand. Either way, Yuwipi is a very popular religion among the Sioux.

A need for a strong, personal relationship with a supernatural force is evidenced in the Plains vision quest. It was incumbent upon each male member of the tribe, upon coming of age, to seek a secluded spot, usually atop a hill or mountain, and stay there fasting and praying until he received a vision, which imparted to him a certain power or set of instructions by which he would live for the rest of his life or until he received new instructions through a later vision.

The vision was essentially a direct communication between man and the supernatural. The form the supernatural took in the vision varied from one individual to another. In his vision the Indian might be visited by a human spirit or that of an animal or bird or even some inanimate object, such as a rock or cloud. He might assume the spirit as his personal charm, or guardian spirit; if visited by a bird he might wear or carry the skin or feathers of that bird to invoke its powers.

Most of the religious, war, and social societies had their origins in visions. Individuals were instructed by spirits to organize various associations and were also told what kind of paraphernalia, emblems, songs, and dances should be used. A man who did not understand

(Smithsonian Institution)
An Indian from the Fort Belknap Reservation, Montana—either Assiniboine or Gros Ventre. This was taken by Sumner W. Matteson in July, 1906. He is a member of the Fool Dancers Society, also called clown makers by other Northern Plains tribes.

the nature of his vision or the instructions given in it might consult an older shaman for an interpretation.

Among many of the Plains tribes, if a person dreamed of thunder or lightning, he was obligated to live out the rest of his life in an antinatural manner. Sometimes called clowns, these men were obligated to perform acts and deeds contrary to what might be expected of the normal person. For example, in the wintertime they went about wearing practically no clothing, claiming that it was hot, and in the summer they wore heavy buffalo robes, complaining of the severe cold. They laughed when they were sad, cried when they were happy, and often spoke backwards.

They were noted for one important ceremony in which they danced around a kettle of meat, plunging their hands in the boiling-hot water to pick out choice portions, claiming that the water was cold. While their actions caused great amusement among the people, it was understood that these men were forced to act abnormally because of their religious convictions. Those who did not act ridiculously believed that they would be struck by lightning.

Important also in the religious life of the Plains Indian was the Sweat Lodge ceremony, one which combined physical and spiritual rejuvenation. Sweat lodges varied somewhat in size and method of construction from one tribe to another, but they were basically dome-shaped dwellings made from willow saplings stuck in the ground around the circumference of the dwelling, bent over, and tied in the center. Inside the lodge a pit was dug to hold a number of rocks, which were heated outside the lodge. The willows were covered with buffalo robes, then blankets and canvass, so that the lodge was as airtight as possible. Once the Indians had crawled into the lodge and took their positions, the rocks were handed in through the doorway by means of special wooden paddles and placed in the pit. After all rocks were in place, the door was covered and the leader of the ceremony spilled cups of water onto the white-hot rocks to produce the steam. The participants often slapped themselves with buffalo tail whips or willow sticks to circulate their blood. The sweat lodge was, in effect, an Indian version of the sauna, or steam bath. At the conclusion of the ceremony the participants wiped their perspiring bodies with sage and plunged into a nearby stream or river. The Crow practiced this even in the wintertime, sometimes breaking the ice in order to submerge themselves.

Big Medicine, Takes Himself, and Fog in the Morning, Crow Indians from Montana outside sweat lodge. The date and photographer were not recorded.

(Smithsonian Institution)

While the Sweat Lodge had many salutory benefits, the main reason for the ceremony was religious in nature. While the doorway of the lodge was closed the participants prayed and sang in loud voices.

I have had the opportunity to participate in the Sweat Lodge ceremony a number of times as an observer, fire tender, and actual participant inside the lodge and found the experience indeed a rewarding one.

The occasion upon which I first participated was in 1966 among the Sioux of Pine Ridge. I was there doing research on their native religion and during my stay came down with a virus, which produced a slight fever. I told my friend and informant, George Plenty Wolf, the leading shaman of the community, about my discomfort, and he suggested that we "sweat" in the late afternoon, when it began to get cool.

I arrived at the sweat lodge, which was located in the backyard of the house of Charles Red Cloud, the recognized chief of the Oglala. Some men had already begun chopping wood and boards for a huge bonfire. Sandstone rocks, brought from the Badlands, were placed in a special pit, and wood was placed around them. One of the men saturated the wood with kerosene and lighted it. As the fire burned the men began to collect blankets and rugs and spread them over the willow frame of the lodge. The lodge itself was small, big enough to accommodate six to eight people. The fire pit inside the lodge was extremely large, measuring 2 feet in depth and about the same in diameter. Sage was spread around the lodge to provide a place to sit.

Plenty Wolf arrived shortly, carrying his pipe and pipe bag. We sat talking while the fire burned. It took almost an hour for the rocks to reach the ideal temperature—white-hot! When the rocks were ready, Plenty Wolf filled the pipe ceremonially, capping the bowl with a sprig of sage, and laid it on a small mound of earth opposite the doorway of the lodge. He signaled to me that it was time to disrobe and enter the lodge. The rest of the men had left except for one young man named Yellow Bull, who was to serve as the fire tender. It was his job to hand the hot rocks in through the doorway and place them in the pit. For this purpose he used a pitchfork.

Sitting cross-legged inside the lodge, with Plenty Wolf directly opposite me, it became apparent that there was little room between myself and the fire pit; the lodge was even smaller than I had judged. Yellow Bull sometimes handed in two or three rocks at the same time, all balanced precariously on the pitchfork. The heat began to build up, even before any water had been added. It seemed that Yellow Bull had an unending supply of rocks back in the fire pit, and I wondered if he would ever stop bringing them in. The small lodge got hotter and hotter, and both Plenty Wolf and I were dripping with sweat—and still the door had to be closed and the water poured over the rocks.

Finally, to my relief, the last rock was put in place, and Yellow Bull handed in a pot of water and tin drinking cup, which he placed next to Plenty Wolf. Plenty Wolf signaled for the door flap to be closed.

The lodge was dark except for a dull glow from the rocks. Plenty Wolf dipped the tin cup into the pot of water and spilled a few drops onto the rocks. I felt before me a sudden rush of steam, as if someone had suddenly opened the door of a blast furnace a few inches

from my face. The heat was unbearable, but more was
to come.

Plenty Wolf then spilled water on the rocks three
more times, four being a sacred number. Then he
began to pray in a rapid voice, which trailed off into
low monotonous tones at the end of each phrase.

The heat emanating from the fire pit was so unbearable that I tried to back up against the lodge to put as
much distance between myself and the rocks as possible.
But I found that the willow saplings supporting the
lodge were so hot that they burned my back. Plenty
Wolf must have sensed my discomfort, because he told
me to lie down and place my face against the ground. I
buried my face in the sage, but there was little relief.
But this time my virus attack and fever seemed to be
totally irrelevant to the situation. I would have welcomed the relative coolness of a fever!

After what seemed to be an eternity of prayers,
Plenty Wolf called to Yellow Bull to open the door
flap. As the blankets were pulled back a gust of fresh
air immediately filled the lodge. I gulped it in, filling
my lungs and welcoming the breeze against my face.
Plenty Wolf filled the cup, took a few sips of water,
and poured the rest over his head. He filled the cup and
handed it to me. I did the same. Never before had air
and water been so important. We sat there for a few
moments relishing the breeze, but by the time I had
become comfortable, Plenty Wolf ordered the door flap
to be shut again. Again he dipped water onto the rocks
and in a few moments the lodge was back to its unbearable norm. The second session was much like the
first, and again, just at the point where I felt I could
take no more and strongly contemplated tearing back

the blanket covering and running out into the cool air, the door flap was opened. There were four sessions in all, the first two being longer than the second two. After the door flap was opened the third time, Yellow Bull lit the pipe and passed it in for us to smoke. The last time, the water was passed around, and the ceremony was concluded.

When I crawled outside the lodge I felt light-headed, as if a magnetic force was trying to pull my body up into the sky. I rubbed myself with sage and lay leaning against the lodge for a moment. The fever was gone. Plenty Wolf chuckled at my relief in being out of the lodge. "It was too hot," he said and chuckled some more.

I was glad he had said it and not I.

To people living close to nature, the sun, moon, and stars, as well as other natural elements, have always figured prominently in their religious beliefs. Likewise, among all early peoples, the human sacrifice has been regarded as the ultimate offering to the deities. The combination of sun worship and human sacrifice is most conspicuous in the Sun dance of the Plains Indians, a religious ceremony which many scholars consider the most important of all Plains rituals.

Much is known about the early Sun dances of the major Plains tribes through the paintings of Catlin and other artists. Further documentation was made through the combined efforts of several anthropologists who researched the Sun dance among the Northern Plains tribes in the early 1900's under the auspices of the American Museum of Natural History. Their findings were later published by the museum in the Anthropological Papers series, which is still available in most public libraries.

While the Sun dance differed in ritual from one tribe to another, there were certain characteristics found in all tribes. The Sun dance was held in the summertime and provided an opportunity for the many scattered bands of one tribe to assemble together in one place. The ritual of the ceremony often took several weeks for preparation, and many days was spent in numerous societal ceremonies, which led up to the Sun dance proper. The reason for Sun dancing was most often attributed to a vow taken by a man or woman who promised to sponsor the dance or participate in it in fulfillment of this vow. The vow was very often made during the thick of battle, when a warrior might proclaim under duress that if his war party escaped annihilation by the enemy, he would perform the Sun dance as a form of thanksgiving. The vow was always made

1967 Oglala Sioux Sun dance, Pine Ridge, South Dakota. Group of men singers.

(Paul Steinmetz, S.J.)

Procession of Sun dancers leaving the sacred tipi.

publicly, and the person making the vow was obligated to fulfill it or risk being ridiculed by his fellow tribesmen.

While there were numerous secondary ceremonies, the highlight of the Sun dance was the portion in which those who had made a vow assembled before the rest of the tribe and danced to the sun. There were many forms of the Sun dance; the dancer might simply dance in place, gazing directly into the sun from sunrise to sunset. But the most spectacular was that portion of the ceremony in which the dancer permitted himself to be pierced by a shaman and strung up to a pole, where he danced until his flesh broke. There were sev-

Raising the sacred pole at the Sun dance.
(Paul Steinmetz, S.J.)

eral ways in which this torture was effected. A shaman would insert a knife into the breast (or both breasts) of the dancer and insert through the flesh a wooden skewer. To the skewer was attached a rawhide rope which in turn was attached to a central "sacred" pole, or in some cases a special frame of poles. The dancer would then dance, pulling back against the rope until the flesh tore. Sometimes, dancers might actually be suspended from the ground by the strength of their flesh. They would literally hang suspended until the weight of their own bodies tore the flesh. Often, a comrade would rush into the center of the dance ring and grab onto a dancer, thus adding his own weight and causing the flesh to break more quickly. Later the dancer who had tortured himself would give away a horse to the friend who had shortened the ordeal.

In another form of the Sun dance, the dancer might have skewers inserted into the flesh over his shoulder blades, which would be attached to a short rawhide rope, one end of which was tied to a buffalo skull. It was necessary for the dancer to walk through the village dragging the buffalo skull behind him until the flesh broke from the weight of the skull. Often, more than one skull was dragged. People sometimes encouraged their children to jump on the skulls and ride behind the dancer, thus adding their weight and causing the flesh to break more quickly.

Sun dance leader, George Plenty Wolf, praying before raising the sacred pole.

(Paul Steinmetz, S.J.)

Dancer whose flesh has been pierced dances pulling against rope until the skin breaks and he is free.

All forms of the Sun dance were rigorous, for the dancers were required to dance from sunup to sundown, with no food or water. Even the simplest form of gazing at the sun required a great deal of stamina.

Although the Sun dance was prohibited by the Federal Government at the close of the nineteenth century, it was reinstated by many of the tribes in the 1930's, without the torture ceremonies. Then in 1959 the Federal Government permitted the Indians to dance the complete form of the dance. In each case, it was the responsibility of the tribal council to determine whether or not the torture ceremony would be permitted. Since 1959 at least two tribes, the Plains Ojibwa at the Turtle Mountain Reservation and the Sioux at the Pine Ridge and Rosebud Reservations have been dancing the complete form of the dance.

I was on hand to witness at the Pine Ridge Reservation the first time the torture ceremony was performed since the turn of the century. The dancer was a middle-aged Sioux man who had left the reservation to work as a plumber's assistant in the city of Pierre, South Dakota. Recently a niece of his had contracted polio. He had vowed that if she recovered from the illness, he would dance the Sun dance and allow himself to be pierced. As it happened, the niece recovered, and he was bound by his vow. He traveled to Pine Ridge, consulted a shaman, and made plans for the event. There were thousands of Sioux from many of the South Dakota reservations to witness the event. After several days of preparation, the Sun dance arbor and sacred pole were erected, and a special tipi set up, where the shaman and dancers would pray before the dance began. Next to the tipi a sweat lodge was built. Before any of the ceremonies started, the shaman, main dancer, and other dancers who were participating to a lesser degree partook of a sweat bath as the sun came up. The Sun dance was performed in a somewhat abbreviated form; the dance was done only from sunrise to noon for three days. The piercing took place on the third day.

The dancer was taken to the center of the dance area and laid down with his head facing the sacred pole.

Sun dancers, wearing wreaths of sage around their heads and circular pendant necklaces, blow on eagle bone whistles tipped with eagle plumes for the duration of the dance.

The shaman took out an awl and made an incision in the dancer's breast. Then the shaman inserted a piece of sinew through the flesh and tied the sinew to a rawhide rope. The dancer stood up and walked backward until the rawhide rope was stretched tautly between his body and the sacred pole. There was a stillness in the audience as the dancer began to bob up and down, blowing on an eagle bone whistle as he gazed directly into the sun. He had danced for about twenty minutes when all of a sudden the rope broke free from his flesh, springing back toward the pole. There was a sigh of relief from the spectators as the shaman approached the dancer and applied Indian medicine to his wound. With that, the dance was concluded, but the torture ceremony was to be performed again and again by others. In 1967 no less than nine dancers were pierced at the Pine Ridge

Sun dance, and there was news that similar Sun dances were being held on other reservations.

I had the opportunity to talk to one of my Sioux friends after he had finished piercing. He had invited me to his camp to talk.

"I wanted to give you this," he said as I arrived. He carefully coiled the rope which had fastened him to the pole and presented it to me. Instead of the old rawhide rope, it was a clothesline which had been painted red. "It's for good luck."

I thanked him and sat down. He touched his breast tenderly and shook his head.

"You know," he said, "it really hurt. I didn't think I could make it. Then I started to really pray, and pretty soon it broke."

"What did you pray for?" I asked.

"All the people," he replied. "Indians and whites,

Sioux Sun dance in progress on the Pine Ridge Reservation. The men in foreground wear traditional kilts made from Hudson's Bay shawls. Offerings of colored cloth are placed next to the sacred pole.

(O'Neill Photo)

everybody. I prayed that the war would end in Vietnam, that all the Indian boys would get home safe."

"Will you dance again next year?" I asked.

He thought for a moment and again touched his breast.

"Yes, I will," he finally answered, "for all the people."

For all the people, I pondered.

Despite the fact that the Indian has been influenced by Christian missionaries for more than a century, it appears that he must turn to his own native religion, even in the twentieth century, to fulfill his spiritual needs. And even though there is some dispute between the Indians themselves as to whether or not the Sun dance has been reinstated strictly for the tourists, it would appear that the individual dancer is very sincere about why he dances and inflicts torture upon himself. Pagan ritual? Call it what you may, but I keep the red rope in my home, not so much for good luck, but as a constant reminder that the Indian religion is still very much alive today. Whatever the method of prayer, it would appear that one which is performed "for all the people" is a valid one.

7 Arts and Crafts

DECORATIVE ART served to enhance the objects which were part of the workaday world of Plains Indian society. Virtually everything men, women, and children owned, from clothing and weapons to cooking utensils and religious paraphernalia, was decorated with painstaking diligence.

Not only was decoration applied to functional objects—dwellings, bows and arrows, moccasins, spoons, and the like, but the mere act of decorating objects rendered them more useful or significant beyond the sphere of pure aesthetics. Objects used in ceremonial life, for instance, become more sacred because of their particular kind of decoration; common household objects became more valuable as trade items if they were highly ornamented. Decoration also served as a form of identification. Certain people were known by the symbols painted on their shields or tipis; certain war societies were known by the way they decorated their costumes or weapons. Historic events and personal deeds were often recorded by means of pictograph drawings on hides and dwellings.

In a society lacking light industry and mass production facilities, naturally everything was hand-made from raw materials found within its geographic boundaries. While, generally speaking, each member of a tribe was expected to contribute to the manufacture of his household and personal belongings, certain people were especially gifted in making bows and arrows, drums, headdresses, and other articles. Thus, apart from the everyday craftsmen, there was a special group of artisans within the tribe known for their ability to manufacture or decorate highly specialized objects.

The artisan was an important member of the tribal society. While in theory any male member of the tribe might be able to construct, say, a drum, the specialist was called upon to make a drum with a certain tone that was considered ideal. The artist, in short, was able to perfect his product. Likewise, while all women attended to the manufacture of their families' dwellings and clothing, some women were especially well-known for their ability to cut clothing patterns or create intricate designs which were more appealing to the wearer. These artists were often compensated through barter and trade for their services.

The amount of time taken to produce an article was based on its immediate need and the work schedule of the artisan. The craftsman did not necessarily spend all of his time at his craft, for he was also expected to participate in all the functions of the tribe. An artisan was not bound by a time clock to work so many hours a day. He would take his time selecting his raw materials, preparing them, making the object, and then decorating it. It was, of course, the results of his craftsmanship by which he was known, not necessarily his techniques or the speed with which he produced his goods. His deadline was essentially self-imposed, not one predetermined by his employer. These aspects of the Indian crafts-man's life are especially important to note: his lack of industrialization, his fame as an individualist and spe-cialist, and his lack of concern with the time involved in making an object. It was precisely these aspects which caused a decline in Indian arts and crafts in later years after the white man had unsuccessfully tried to impose his work standards on the Indian society.

Specialists in the material culture of the Plains Indian generally agree that the year 1850 marked a historical dividing line between the traditional methods of manu-facture and decoration and the use of newly introduced trade goods by the white man. The pre-1850 era is sometimes called the hide period to denote the pre-dominance of animal skins, such as buffalo, elk, and deer, in the manufacture of clothing. After 1850, cloth, beads, and other trade goods became widely diffused among all the Plains tribes. There were basically two methods of diffusion: direct contact with the white trad-ers at their isolated trading posts, or forts, and indirect contact, in which an intermediary tribe carried trade goods from the white men to other tribes. In many in-stances, Plains tribes became acquainted with European trade items before ever seeing a white man.

Before 1850 the everyday clothing of the Indian man consisted of a loincloth, leggings, and moccasins, to which might be added a poncho-type shirt or a buffalo robe, depending on the season and occasion. Some clothing was worn everyday, while fine clothing and costumes were worn only on festive or ceremonial occa-sions. The Indians generally wore only feathers and other symbols of achievements or status at public func-tions or on the warpath.

Women wore long, ankle-length dresses—usually made of elkskins or deerskins—knee-length leggings, and moccasins. Children wore clothing similar to the adults'.

The most widely used garment "fabric" of the Plains Indian was buckskin. Technically, buckskin is any kind of deer- or elkskin which has been scraped clean of flesh and hair and has been softened. Tanning the skins was the job of the women. A green skin was first soaked in water and a solution of ashes for several days. Then it was stretched and staked to the ground, and the hair and flesh were removed with a bone scraper—later replaced by metal skinning knives. The woman then rubbed a mixture of brains and grease into the skin and rubbed it in her hands or over a rough board until the skin became pliable. Some tribes preferred to smoke their buckskin over a pit fire, which gave the skin a darker color. If desired, the hair might be left on and only the flesh side tanned. The finished product was—and still is—referred to as Indian tan buckskin, to differentiate it from chemically tanned leather used in the commercial market for coats and gloves.

Rawhide, the state of the skin which has been fleshed and dehaired but not tanned, was also used in the manufacture of mocassin soles, shields, drums, and parfleche boxes. When rawhide dries, it is extremely hard and durable. It shrinks to some degree, making it useful for binding tomahawk heads and other utensils securely.

To sew buckskin and rawhide, Plains women used sinew, a tendon found along the backbones of buffalo and other animals, for thread. A hole was punctured by means of a bone awl and the sinew inserted. The tip of the sinew was usually whetted and rolled into a sharp point. When it dried, it had a durable, needlelike point. The sinew wore like iron, often outlasting the buckskin and rawhide to which it was sewn. Sinew was also used for binding arrowheads to the shafts.

Generally speaking, at one time each tribe living on

Wolf Plume, Curly Bear, and Bird Rattler, Blackfeet of Browning, Montana. This was taken in 1916 by De Lancey Gill of the Bureau of American Ethnology. The two men on the right are wearing Blackfeet "straight up" bonnets.

(Smithsonian Institution)

the Northern Plains could be identified by the kinds
of clothing and costuming its members wore. The
greatest difference was not so much the cut and design,
but the decoration and ornamentation. The farther back
in history we go, the greater distinction there was in
tribal styles, but as we progress we find that a great exchange of ideas occurred among the tribes which affected
their styles of dress. Before the reservation period,
many tribes were trading with one another, bartering one
tribal style for another. When the French and English
traders appeared, they traded the same kinds of items
with all tribes, so that a great similarity in clothing and
costume began to be established.

The period in which each tribe dressed differently
from the next might be called the classical period of
Indian dress. In this period we would expect to find a
Blackfeet warrior wearing a "straight up" eagle feather
warbonnet, while a Sioux wore one which swept backward from the forehead, often trailing to the ground.
The Cree and other tribes closely affiliated with Woodland Indians wore moccasins which were made entirely
of buckskin. Other tribes wore the more typical hard-sole
moccasins, which were constructed with buckskin tops
and rawhide soles.

The earlier clothing was rather simple in pattern and
construction. Men's leggings were often made of two
deerskins—one for each leg—simply folded in half and
tacked along the seam. A poncho-type shirt was made of
two skins sewn together; a robe was made of an entire
buffalo skin. An Indian woman lucky enough to have
two matching elkskins could make a complete dress. It
usually took about five deerskins to make the same
dress, because deerskins were smaller. Because tanning

skins took a great deal of time and effort, Indian women were especially conservative in their cutting of skins. Each remnant was kept for smaller articles of clothing or patching skins.

While there was great similarity in patterns of clothing during the classical period, there was a great difference in design and ornamentation. Before 1850 decoration took the form of painted designs and porcupine quillwork. Paints were made of vegetable, nut, and mineral dyes, and designs were applied with bone or wood brushes. Quillwork was much more complicated and desirable. First the quills were removed from the porcupine, a delicate task to avoid being pricked by its barbed points. The quills were then dyed to the desired color and dried. Before starting, the woman flattened each quill with her teeth and held the quills in her mouth as she worked. There were a variety of ways the quills were applied to the buckskin clothing. They were most often overlapped in neat rows and sewn in place with sinew. Often the quills were simply wrapped around a rawhide strip and several strips sewn together to form armbands or quilled fringe for pipe bags. Quills were also wrapped around buckskin thongs to serve as ornamentative dangles which hung from various articles of clothing and costuming. They were also plaited and used to decorate handles of tomahawks and pipestems.

Painting most often took the form of pictograph drawings, semi-realistic pictures which were used to record battle deeds or other exploits in the life of a man. Men signed their names, usually by drawing the pictograph of a man's head and directly over it a picture representing his name. Sitting Bull, the great

Sioux leader, signed his name by drawing a pictograph
of a seated buffalo over the outline of a head. He also
kept very elaborate records of his battles with other
Indian tribes, as well as the United States Cavalry.
Figures which are depicted upside down on his records
represent enemies slain. His records have been published in two volumes by the Smithsonian Institution.

Several years ago I obtained a ceremonial whip from
the Sioux which contained several interesting pictographs applied to the wooden handle by means of a
black crayon. The pictographs enumerated some of the
outstanding deeds of the whip's owner. One sequence of
drawings told how he had gone on a long horse-stealing
foray. There was an *X* accompanied by three slashes

Pictograph describing a buffalo hunting scene drawn by the
Cheyenne, Making Medicine.

(Smithsonian Institution)

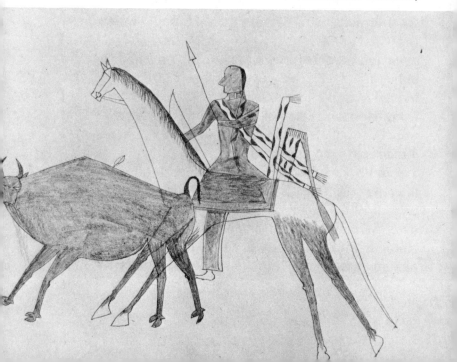

which indicated he had camped (the X represented the campfire) three nights on the trail. His success in capturing horses was indicated by three horseshoelike symbols. It also showed how his own horse had been wounded by means of a horseshoe with a hole in the center of it, from which emanated a stream of blood. Other symbols showed that he had earned the right to smoke the pipe, sit in important councils, and that he had participated in some of the major Sioux ceremonies. On the reverse side of the whip handle was a long zigzag figure running the length of the whip, which symbolized a bolt of lightning. Upon inquiring about its significance, I was told that it was there as a constant reminder to the whip owner that if he lied about any of the deeds depicted on the reverse side, he would be killed by lightning.

One of the most interesting and historically valuable forms of pictograph recording is the winter count. This was a type of calendar on which each important event of the year was recorded on a piece of skin and kept by one man until he died. Each symbol served as a mnemonic device to assist the keeper to relate the important historical events of his band or tribe. In most cases, the symbols were intelligible only to the keeper. In order to pass it on, he taught his son or some close friend or relative how to read the count. Too often the information contained on the calendar passed on with its keeper.

Fortunately, some of the early anthropologists, and even some Indians who recognized the importance of preserving the winter counts, collected and translated them. I was fortunate to have secured from an old Sioux named John Colhoff, or White Man Stands in

Sight, as he was known by his people, a winter count allegedly kept by a member of the Bad Face band of the Oglala. The first entry in this account dates from 1759. Colhoff spent much time with the original keeper before he died and recorded the meanings of the pictographs in both English and Lakota.

The original entries were painted on a buffalo hide, the first entry being made in the center of the skin and the others placed in a spiraling line around the center one. Later, some were kept on canvas or cotton cloth, and the drawing and placement of the entries varied.

The Bad Face winter count listed 1759 as the year "different bands of the Sioux had scattered out. This is supposed to have happened between the Mississippi and Missouri river plains." Most of the entries are concerned with famous men who died or were killed by enemies and with glorious accomplishments on the warpath. However, other pictographs tell of the numerous epidemics of smallpox and measles which raged through the Sioux band. Many students of Indian history enjoy using the winter counts for comparing Indian records with those published in non-Indian sources. In many cases there are discrepancies, but quite often one source corroborates the other. In the Bad Face count, for example, Colhoff writes for the entry 1833: "Storm of stars. Shooting stars like snow flakes in a storm. This checks the white man's history when flying meteors sprayed North America into the Atlantic Ocean on November 13, 1833."

It must be remembered that the pictograph entry was comprised of one or two semirealistic drawings which served simply to spark the memory of its keeper. The keeper had to have an exceptional ability to remember detail. Most of the entries in the Bad Face count are very precise about the number of men killed in battle, and often their names are included. One of the most famous incidents in Sioux history is recorded for 1854. Colhoff writes:

Chief Conquering Bear was killed. This was near Ft. Laramie, just inside of Nebraska on the Platte River. The Mormons left a crippled cow on the trail. Two Lakotas killed the cow after trading for it, so it was claimed by the two Indians who killed it. "Wase" and "Itohe woga" were the two—Paint and Pompador. When the Mormons reached Ft. Laramie, they complained to the commanding officer about the cow. The officer at once sent a troop of cavalry to the Indian village to make an arrest of guilty parties.

Lt. John L. Gratton with 29 men and an interpreter came to Chief Conquering Bear's Lodge and demanded the chief to give up the guilty parties.

The chief said that he couldn't do that at once because at that time he didn't know anything about it.

The Lakotas gathered here from all parts for their annual worship, The Sun Dance, so that there were many bands. But the officer and his interpreter insisted vigorously.

Conquering Bear told them that he could not do this at present.

Then the officer said fire! and Chief Conquering Bear fell dead in his tracks. It was like poking a hornets nest. None of the soldiers got out of the camp circle, they were all killed within a few yards of each other except the interpreter, who had a fast horse, and almost got away. One shot broke the horses front leg and the man fell. When the Lakotas got to him, he begged for mercy, but it was too late, he fell with hundreds of arrows in his body.

Lastly, one warrior arrived a little late. He said, "You made a remark in front of Conquering Bear. You had plenty of bullets for me. I have none for you but this tomahawk."

And he drew back and struck the man deep into his brains and left it in his head.

"Take that along with you," he said.

The popularity of pictographic art and, to some degree, porcupine quillwork, began to wane after 1850, largely because of new and more easily accessible trade goods. Convenience was a determining factor. It was much easier to make clothing from the wool cloth brought by the traders. Trade, or list, cloth, as it was known, became very popular as a material for loincloths, leggings, and blankets, slowly replacing the traditional skin garments. Cotton cloth, calico, and gingham were perfect for making shirts and dresses. Readymade items, such as pants, shirts, vests, and coats, could now be obtained from the traders or at the military forts. Clothing and costuming of the Plains tribes slowly began to take on new dimensions, sometimes comical ones, for the Indians were eager to trade for anything. Old photographs show tribal delegations on their way to Washington, D.C., wearing moccasins, leggings, blankets, homemade shirts, and beaver hats. This was also a period in which the Indian tribes who had come in contact with the white man began to imitate much of what he did—including what he wore. The mark of civilization was

Crow Indian woman in ceremonial dress leading procession at the Crow Indian Fair, Crow Agency, Montana. Notice the elaborately beaded dress and horse trappings.
(Bureau of Indian Affairs)

essentially determined by the cut of a man's clothing. Many of the Indians saw fit to comply with the white man's concept of civility.

Other items of trade had an even more substantial effect on the art of the Plains Indian. Probably the most influential item of trade was the glass bead. Heretofore the Plains Indians had made beads from stone, bone, and shell or had traded for them with other tribes to the east and west. Now there was an opportunity to obtain beads of European manufacture which were uniform in size and color and could be secured in great abundance.

The early beads were large and came for the most

part from Venice. Carrie Lyford, writing in "Quill and Beadwork of the Western Sioux," described this bead:

> From about 1800 to 1840 a large opaque irregular china bead came into use on the Plains. It was known as the pony bead because it was brought in by the pony pack trains. The pony bead was made in Venice. It was about ⅛ inch in diameter, about twice as large as the beads used later. White and a medium sky blue were the colors in which the pony beads were commonly used. Black pony beads also appeared in the old pieces. A few deep buff, light and dark red, and dark blue pony beads have also been noted.

After 1840 a smaller bead came into prominence. This was sometimes called a seed bead. Later translucent and faceted, or cut, beads were introduced. The Indians sometimes differentiate between seed and glass beads; however, they are both made of glass. The difference is that seed (opaque) beads are colored after they are blown, while glass beads are blown from a precolored substance. Metallic beads were also introduced by the traders.

As in quillwork, which beadwork was inevitably destined to replace, there were a variety of beading techniques. The most popular were spot, or overlay, stitch and a technique especially popular among the Crow, Cheyenne, Arapaho, and Sioux, called lazy stitch.

Overlay stitch, a technique known among non-Indians as couching, was a method of beading in which two threads were used, one to string the beads, the other to sew the string of beads to the garment. This was basically a technique employed to sew quillwork and was easily adaptable to beadwork. Overlay stitch, recognizable by long, flat lines covering the surface of an article, was especially popular among the Blackfeet, Sarsi, Plains Cree, Crow, Assiniboine, Gros Ventre, and Eastern Sioux. This technique was especially adaptable for beading floral designs.

Lazy stitch, sometimes called hump stitch because of its peculiar contour when applied to flat pieces, was especially good for covering large surfaces of garments with relative speed. In this method, only one thread was used. The sinew was knotted and inserted through the buckskin; six or eight beads were strung on and sinew inserted partially through, or caught, in the buckskin. The beads were sewn back and forth in neat rows. When the beadwork was pulled tight the row arched slightly; hence, the name hump stitch. The term lazy stitch probably came from the fact that it was much easier and quicker than overlay.

In early times, the beadwork was done exclusively with sinew. Later cotton thread and especially fine beading needles were introduced to the Plains tribes. Sinew continued to be used, for the most part, to apply beadwork to buckskin, but thread was more ideal for sewing beads to cloth.

The years 1860–1900 were the great age of beadwork, and there was good reason for it. The Plains tribes which once roamed the Plains in pursuit of game and new camping areas were now living the sedentary reservation life. Indian women now had more time to attend to sewing and decorating their clothing and costumes. This was the period in which not only clothing and costuming received great attention, but such items as cradleboards, horse trappings, household furniture

Old Blackfeet woman wearing cloth dress and silver trade earrings. Photographed around 1900. *(Smithsonian Institution)*

and ceremonial paraphernalia were decorated with painstaking care. Beadwork reached a point where one might even say that it was overdone from the viewpoint of comfort; Indian dresses contained so much beadwork that they often weighed forty to fifty pounds!

There were other trade items that greatly influenced Indian decorative art. In addition to seed beads, there was a variety of large glass and brass "trade" beads, which were used for necklaces and fringes. Brass studs used by the white people to decorate their horse trappings were used by the Indians to ornament tack belts; a finely made tubular bone bead and bone hair pipe were manufactured by the Europeans for the Indian trade and served as the foundations of bone breastplates and other forms of necklaces and chokers. German silver conchos and ball and cone earrings were popular on the Plains. The Indians used trade conchos and later handwrought ones to make various hair decorations called hair plates, and concho belts. Bells were in great demand. Large brass sleigh bells were used by the dancers on their legs, and smaller hawk bells were used to decorate various parts of the dancers' costumes.

Not only did trade items change the Indians' decorative techniques, but elements of traditional design began to take a new look. As has been stated, pictographic art was done in a semirealistic style. Porcupine quillwork for the most part, was done in geometric designs, but some attempt at floral and realistic styles was also made by expert craftsmen. It has been often erroneously stated that geometric design was indigenous to the Plains, while floral designs were concentrated among

Sioux Indian women from McLaughlin, South Dakota, in full dress. Note the large "hair pipe" breastplates worn over the trade cloth dresses. This photo possibly was taken by K. L. Hatch in 1921.

(Smithsonian Institution)

Little Bear, an Arapaho Indian. Bureau of American Ethnology photographer F. A. Rinehart photographed this man at the Omaha Exposition in 1898. His shirt is made from an American flag. The front apron is decorated with typical floral beadwork.

the Woodland tribes. Actually both forms of design were found on the Northern Plains. As a general rule, however, geometric designs were in abundance in the central Plains, while floral designs were found predominantly among the Northernmost tribes and those tribes which were closest to the Woodland tribes. There was an uncommon blend of both styles among the Crow.

When beadwork made its appearance on the Plains, Indian women began to adapt quillwork designs and those found on painted parfleche boxes.

Originally, geometric designs were limited to large blocklike shapes, but as Indian craftsmen became proficient with the new materials, their designs became more varied and intricate; triangles, step patterns, forked designs, crosses, and combinations of these basic patterns became predominant. It has also been suggested by the late F. H. Douglas, curator of the Denver Art Museum's Indian collection, that some beadwork designs were actually influenced by rugs made in the Caucasus, which were common in American households after 1870.

Floral beadwork simply depicted, in a semi-realistic way, leaves and flowers common to the vicinity. There is no question that many floral designs were simply copied by the Plains tribes from their Woodland neighbors.

In the later period there was a great deal of beadwork which contained realistic designs, mostly of men and horses, which were reminiscent of the earlier pictographs. With the surge of patriotism related to World War I, it was common to see, especially among the Sioux, designs containing abstractions of the American flag and eagle. Photographs from this period bear out that it was also considered patriotic to fashion shirts and shawls from American flags to wear at public functions.

Designs were generally the domain of the woman. The Indian woman usually made up the designs as she worked; patterns were not generally used. Favorite designs were sometimes repeated on various articles, and certain women became well-known for their treatments of line and color. Much has been written about the symbolism of Indian designs; however, by and large, the Indian woman created her designs because they were aesthetically pleasing to her. Design elements which were used often were sometimes given names, such as arrow design or hill design, but there was very little symbolic significance to the arrangement of these designs in the finished work.

Mrs. Gray Eagle and grandchild, Sioux. Some of the very old women still dress this way. Photo by Bell. *(Courtesy John Colhoff)*

Indian arts and crafts are still very much a part of the Plains Indian way of life, even though some of the older traditional techniques have been slowly disappearing. Cotton thread has all but replaced sinew; however, sinew-sewn work is still considered the best and demands a higher price than thread-sewn wares. Indian tanning has become all but obsolete because of the prevalence of chemically tanned skins, which are uniform in color and weight. Buckskin costumes of today are often sewn on sewing machines. Quillwork is quickly becoming a dying art, despite some sporadic attempts to rejuvenate it. Indian children are learning new Euro-American art techniques in school and many have become accomplished artists, working in water color and oil. Old Indian designs which once adorned tipis, shields, and parfleche boxes are often painted on modern homes, and Indian artists are often commissioned to paint native designs on the walls of churches and official government buildings.

Beadwork is probably the most important native craft still practiced on the reservations. White schoolteachers introduced to the Plains tribes the European method of weaving beads called loomwork, and this latter method is nowadays preferred by many over the older overlay and lazy stitch techniques. Beads are still sold by Indian traders or bought through mail-order catalogues.

Indian craftsmen, although they recognize a certain value in the older art forms of their ancestors, readily adapt to new raw materials and techniques of costume work. The dry goods store is a place frequented by Indian men and women to buy such items as sequins, tassles, nylon fringe, fancy embroidery, ribbon, maribou, and costume jewelry, all of which are woven into their dance costumes with Indian uniqueness. Especially on the Northern Plains, the young dancers today wear costumes which contain a mixture of traditional Indian craftwork and a host of baubles and spangles right out of the millinery section of a department store. On many reservations the women have substituted their traditional buckskin dresses with cotton dresses, over which they wear cotton and silk fringed "Indian" shawls, which are purchased in the local stores. The beaded dresses, which are now considered by many too hot

James Mooney took this photograph of Sioux dancers at Pine Ridge, South Dakota, in 1892. The singers are squatting around a commercially made bass drum, still a popular substitute for the traditional rawhide drum.

and heavy, are kept in mothballs and regarded as heirlooms to be worn only on very special occasions.

That is not to say that all traditional forms of art and craft are obsolete. Generally speaking, the farther north you travel on the Plains, the more traditional the arts and crafts remain. In northern Montana and on the Canadian reservations, traditional craftwork is still found in great abundance, and older craft techniques are still practiced. Also, the collectors who have ravaged many of the central Plains reservations have not yet reached the northernmost regions of the Plains.

A relatively small segment of the Indian people make a somewhat modest living making arts and crafts for sale to tourist shops. Some tribal councils have set up Indian craft cooperatives, which allow the people to buy raw materials wholesale and also sell their finished products to stores in volume. Indian-owned craft shops may also be found, such as the Standing Rock Arts and Crafts Guild at Fort Yates, North Dakota, the Arts and Crafts Shop at Pine Ridge, South Dakota, and the Northern Plains Indian Crafts Association at Billings,

Montana. Indians also sell their wares to small shops on busy highways highly traveled by tourists. Some of the best Indian crafts are to be found in small, out-of-the-way stores, such as Hardin's Store in Hardin, Montana, which has a fine collection of Crow craftwork.

On some reservations, such as the Turtle Mountain Reservation in North Dakota, the Northern Cheyenne Reservation in Montana, and at Pine Ridge and Rosebud, South Dakota, arts and crafts are being sustained as a form of light industry. Such items as beadwork, moccasins, traditional craftwork, and "artifakery" (modern reproductions of artifacts) are being produced in volume by tribally owned factories or factories leased by non-Indian manufacturers. Light industry is still in its infancy, as authentic craftwork does not lend itself to mass production; however, some attempt is being made to provide jobs in which Indians can use native skills. It has been somewhat difficult for many Indians to adjust to mass produced craftwork, because most of them feel that items should be made on an individual basis. There is little pride of manufacture in a craft article that has passed through a production line.

With an increasing popularity in Indian craftwork among tourists and organizations such as the Boy Scouts of America and the Y.M.C.A., there has been an overwhelming tide of imitation beadwork and leatherwork. Much has been produced in Hong Kong and Tokyo. Imitiation beadwork is sold through mail-order catalogues and in many tourist shops. Some can even be found on Indian reservations, as Indians can make a greater profit on imitation crafts than they can on their own. Japanese beadwork, for instance, is sold by the yard, an impossibility with handcrafted Indian beadwork.

Realizing a decline in traditional crafts and a surge of foreign-made craftwork, an act of Congress created the Indian Arts and Crafts Board in 1935. Congress charged this agency of the Department of the Interior with policing misrepresentation of authentic Indian crafts and also to assist native craftsmen in the business and promotional aspects of the industry. The board has established numerous field offices on and off reservations which encourage traditional craftwork. It also serves as an outlet through which Indians may sell their products. The board also sponsors Indian arts and crafts shows in many of the larger cities.

Concurrent with the creation of the Indian Arts and Crafts Board, Congress offered the following protection to Indian craftsmen:

Whoever willfully offers or displays for sale any goods, with or without any Government trademark, as Indian products or Indian products of a particular Indian tribe or group, resident within the United States or Territory of Alaska, when such person knows such goods are not Indian products or are not Indian products of the particular Indian tribe or group, shall be fined not more than $500 or imprisoned not more than six months, or both.

In addition to Federal protection, many states in which there are large Indian populations have similar legislation.

It appears that with Federal and state protection for the Indian craftsmen and a resurgence in arts and crafts by the people themselves, native arts, despite changes in raw materials and techniques, will live on for a very long time.

8 Music and Dance

MUSIC AND DANCE were among the most important aspects of early native American life. The Plains Indian had a song for everything he did. Singing was an important part of curing diseases, invoking the spirits, and relating daily events, such as the birth of a child or death of a warrior. There were travel songs, social songs, songs of the Sun dance and other religious events, songs for working, dancing, hunting, and warfare. Each men's society had its own songs, as did the women's organizations. There were songs for individuals and songs for entire choruses.

Dancing was a form of recreation, as well as a dramatic medium through which stories of war and the hunt were told. When a warrior returned from the warpath, he retold his deeds in dance drama and gesture language. There were dances before going on the buffalo hunt to insure success for the hunters, as well as victory dances after a war party had returned successfully from battle. The most significant to the most menial of Plains Indian ceremonialism was replete with music and dance.

Ethnomusicologists, scientists who study the music

of aboriginal peoples and ethnic groups, have organized the music of the Plains Indian into one music area. Since some of the Plains music is related to the music of the Southwest Indians, it is called the Plains-Pueblo music area. It encompasses all tribes of the Northern and Southern Plains, as well as the Pueblo tribes of New Mexico and Arizona. The similarities and differences between the music of these two cultures are obvious only to the trained ear. For most people, all Indian music sounds alike.

The music of this area was characterized by extremely high-pitched singing by the men, especially on the Northern Plains. Injected into the songs were wild animal calls and piercing wails. The women sang along with the men in some songs, a full octave above them. Occasionally the women would sound the ear-splitting tremolo in honor of some brave who had died in battle. This sound is frequently heard in movies as a war cry. It is usually performed by a man who yells loudly and at the same time pats his mouth with an open hand to produce an uluating sound. On the Northern Plains, however, only women produced this sound, and they did it simply by fluttering their tongues against the roofs of their mouths as they wailed. It was considered a womanly form of applause, rather than a war cry.

Indian music of this area is said to be composed on the pentatonic scale; that is, there are five tones to the scale. Most Western music is composed on an eight-tone scale. In this way Indian music is very similar to Chinese and Japanese music and to that of the Mid-East. Most of the music from the Plains is built on what ethnomusicologists call a descending scale; the songs start on a high note and cascade downward to a low note.

Some Indian songs were composed with words; others were made up of meaningless syllables called vocables, or nonsense syllables. Meaningless words served simply to carry the tune and in some cases identify songs. Songs with words might tell of the war deeds of a warrior or his prowess as a hunter. Some honored those slain in battle, while others spoke the mysterious words of the shamans. A few songs were remodeled year after year, adding new words according to the whims of their composers, while others remained unchanged for generations.

Relatively little is known about Northern Plains music before 1870. It was not until the turn of the century that anthropologists armed with sound recording equipment began to collect and preserve Indian songs. It is very likely that many songs survived over the period of time since the Indian roamed the Plains freely, and many songs which exist today may be well over 100 years old. Many kinds of Indian songs became obsolete when the functions they served died. New songs, however, took their place.

The development of ethnomusicology and the collection of American Indian songs on cylinders was spearheaded largely by women; namely, Helen H. Roberts, Alice C. Fletcher, and Frances Densmore. The last was the most prolific writer and has published a number of books on the music of many tribes. Her contribution to the music of the Northern Plains is the now classic "Teton Sioux Music," published by the Bureau of American Ethnology (now the Office of Anthro-

Hunkpapa Sioux singers and dancer, Standing Rock Reservation, North Dakota.
(Bureau of Indian Affairs)

pology). While it contains some musical discrepancies, it is still considered one of the best musical ethnographies of any tribe.

George Herzog was a musicologist usually given credit for defining music styles in the United States, using vocal techniques as a criterion. Much of his work was concerned with describing how certain kinds of Northern Plains music diffused from the Great Basin area.

Certain men were known as good song makers and singers. A good singer had a loud and clear voice, could remember songs easily, had a large repertory of songs, and could learn a new song after hearing it only once or twice. When performing for religious celebrations, singers had to sing the right songs in the proper order, or the ceremony would go unheeded by the Great Spirit.

Inspiration for songs usually came from visions or

dreams. In the vision the singer was instructed in songs, dances, and ceremonies by a supernatural animal or bird. When the man awoke from his vision, it was incumbent upon him to go back to his village and teach other young men what he had seen in the vision.

Other songs were created by the process that ethnomusicologists call conscious composition. An Indian singer would simply decide to compose a song and sit down and hum or whistle certain musical strains to himself until he arrived at what he considered an ideal combination of melody and words or vocables. Like composers around the world, the Indian usually sought a secluded spot, where he could be alone with his artistic inspiration. Often, singers were asked by other members of the tribe to create songs for special functions and were remunerated with horses or other valuable gifts.

While many songs were sung by individuals, such as in the curing rites of the dream societies, other songs were sung by choruses of men and women to the accompaniment of the drum. The large bass drum was played by a group of men who squatted around it, beating it with drumsticks. Others used an ensemble of hand drums, each man beating his own small drum with a drumstick. Farther back in history, a hollowed log or folded rawhide was beaten with a stick.

Only certain singers could lead group songs. They had to have perfect pitch so that the song was not started too high or too low. The leader started a song, thus setting the pitch, after which the rest of the singers joined in singing the part the leader had already sung, then continued on with the song.

An Omaha dance in full swing on the Pine Ridge Indian Reservation, South Dakota. The dance is traditionally performed inside a circular brush arbor. This photo was taken in September, 1945.

Since singers had to provide the music for not only the social, but the religious life of the village, they were respected men of the tribe.

The Indian song maker might sell or trade his songs for articles he needed or for the right to sing other songs. Song swapping is still an important leisure-time activity. One singer sang a tune for me which he said was originally known as the laughing song, because it contained the vocables *ha-ha-ha*. Later, he said, the song was sold to another singer for five dollars and, after that, was known as the five-dollar song. Normally Indian songs had no titles; they were simply referred to as dance songs, curing songs, and the like. After Indians began to record songs commercially, however, they began to give them such colorful names as "The Legend of Lover's Leap," "The Japs Are Crying," and "Korean Memorial Song" (the latter two being songs of World War II and Korea respectively).

There were very few varieties of instruments among the Plains Indians; music was largely vocal. While some music was simply sung with no accompaniment, dance music was usually accompanied by some form of instrument.

The most popular and widespread instrument in all America was the drum. Drums came in a variety of sizes and shapes. There were hand drums and large dance drums. Normally, they were circular in shape, but some were four-sided.

Drums were usually made of hollowed logs covered with an animal hide. They had either one or two heads. Some of the larger drums were supported by elaborate drum racks. Others were held by the singers.

After the Europeans arrived, the shells of drums were made of cheese boxes or barrels and eventually many Indians tried to trade for commercially made bass drums used by the military bands.

The rhythms of the drum on the Plains never reached the sophistication of the Africans or Polynesians. The steady, pulsating rhythms, or drum tremolos, served simply to accompany and emphasize the songs. The song was always the most important part of the ceremony, usually more important than the dance.

Most drumming was comprised of steady, pulsating beats, with few or no accents. The popular LOUD-soft-soft-soft beating often heard on television and in the movies was never really part of Indian music. In the war songs, loud, accented beats interspersed between steady beats imitated gunshots.

Another popular instrument was the rattle. It was made of a rawhide frame filled with pebbles or of the dew claws of the deer, which were strung on a bandolier or stick. Later, when European traders introduced bells, they became an important part of the dancers' costumes. The Sioux say that originally a warrior wore a bell for each time he was wounded. Later, bells were added simply for their sound. They were worn around the dancers' ankles or knees, sometimes hanging from waist to ankles.

Dancers also used various forms of flutes and whistles. The whistles were said to imitate the sounds of the eagle. They were used as signals in warfare and in the dance, especially in the ceremonies of the men's societies.

Sometimes the whistles were elaborately carved. One of the most popular kind among the Gros Ventre, Arikara, and Mandan of North Dakota was carved to resemble the head and beak of a crane.

When courting their sweethearts, young men used a flute, on which they played love songs. In the evening the young man stood far enough from his sweetheart's lodge to remain undetected by a watchful morther or grandmother and played a melody on the flute. The young girl recognized the melody and knew her young man was thinking about her. Courtship, in its early stages, was never out in the open. The young man could wait quietly along a path leading to a stream, and there would call to his sweetheart as she walked by going for water. Sometimes the young buck would be too embarrassed to speak to her, and might only tug at her sleeve and then disappear into the woods. As he grew more confident, he would stop her and talk to her.

If she remained to talk then his chances of seeing her again were good, and he would return to his lodge to compose a melody for the flute.

Indian music is still very much a part of the contemporary Indian's way of life, and hundreds of new songs are composed each year. The Northern Plains represents the center of Indian musical creativity in all of the United States and Canada. Just as there is more emphasis on traditional arts and crafts on the northernmost reservations, especially in Montana and Canada, there appears to be more musical creativity the farther North one travels. Most of the Indian tribes on the Plains agree that the best songs come from Montana and Canada, mainly from the Cree and Canadian Sioux. These new songs are quickly diffused southward from one tribe to another. They are usaully heard at the larger celebrations, especially the Sun dances, which attract members of many tribes. The songs, once heard and learned by the visitors, are carried back to each reservation, where they are sometimes changed slightly and sung in the preferred style of the adapting tribe. Tape recorders are very popular among Indian singers, and many of them make long treks to other reservations to learn and collect new songs and thus shorten the normal channels of diffusion. Even singers from the Southern Plains travel to Montana in the summer to obtain new songs, which they introduce to their own people at the Oklahoma powwows.

Commercial and noncommercial recordings of Indian music have been burgeoning over recent years. There are fine collections in the Library of Congress and the Archives of Traditional Music at Indiana University. Some of the recordings and tapes are used exclusively

The Kettle dance, performed before a feast, was an important part of the Grass dance ceremony. Here, Assiniboine dancers feign their spears at a kettle of dog meat, a delicacy among many Northern Plains tribes. This photo was taken by Sumner W. Matteson at the Fort Belknap Reservation, July, 1906.

for musicological studies in the universities, but even Indians are buying commercial discs of their own music and songs of other tribes, which they play on home phonographs or jukeboxes in the local reservation cafes.

As the Indian sang, so did he dance. While dances were primarily for the Indian men, many of them being centered around the hunt and warfare, there were also dances for women and even children.

The women's dances were usually limited to the special dances of the women's clubs. However, after a band of warriors returned from a skirmish, the women usually performed the Scalp dance, dancing around in a circle, displaying the scalps that the menfolk had taken in battle. They sometimes wore their relatives' war-bonnets, painted their faces black, and carried the scalps suspended from long poles. The Scalp dance has survived but, of course, without the bloody symbols of battle. Today it is danced by men and women alike and is simply called the Round dance.

While in our own society new dances come and go and very rarely last more than one or two years, there was a dance "craze" among the Plains Indians that became so prominent that it lasted more than 100 years and is still being done by practically all tribes. It is called by most the Grass dance.

The Grass dance originated in Nebraska, more than likely among the Pawnee, although it was popularized throughout the Northern Plains tribes by the Omaha and Sioux. Originally the Pawnee called it the Irushka, which referred to a particular kind of headdress worn by the dancers, called the hair roach. Translated, Irushka means "standing in the middle of the fire," and it was symbolic of the single eagle feather attached in the center of the hair roach; the feather represented a man, and the red hair was the fire. This symbolic meaning was soon lost, even though the headdress was retained by all the tribes as an essential part of the Grass dance costume.

The Omaha Indians had a feature of their dance in which they tied bunches of braided grass to their belts to represent scalps. The Omaha taught the dance to the Sioux. Some of the Sioux called the dance the Omaha dance, naming it after the tribe who taught them, while others called it the Grass dance, after the Omaha custom of tying grass to the belts. The dance was then known by the Sioux under two names, the Omaha wacipi (Omaha dance) and Peji Mignaka Wacipi, or "They Dance with Grass Tucked in Their Belts," later shortened to Grass dance.

In addition to the hair roach, dancers wore crow belts, and carried eagle bone whistles. There were many elaborate ceremonies in which certain men of the tribe were invested with the right to wear these articles of costuming.

The dance was held at any flat place within the camp, but later the dance was performed (and still is) in large circular brush arbors. A herald would go around the camp announcing that there would be a Grass dance and that all the people should put on their best clothing, paint their faces, and make ready for the dance. Soon the singers arrived carrying their drum, which they placed on a frame of four sticks.

As the singing started the male members of the tribe stepped out into the center of the dance area and began moving in free-style steps and body motions in time to the song and drumbeat. There was not much emphasis on fancy footwork; most of the movement was with the head and shoulders. The men attempted to make the feathers in their headdresses dance and "wrestle" as they tap-stepped in zigzag lines and small circles around the center of the dance area. The women merely bobbed up and down around the edges of the dance area. At what appeared to be the end of the song, the drum would stop and immediately begin again. This time one man chosen for his ability as a warrior would dance a solo encore called the tail.

Between dances the people gave away horses, tobacco, and blankets to the needy. They gave things to the singers so that the names of relatives killed in battle might be remembered in song.

One of the highlights of the Grass dance was the feast. It usually began in the evening, but before the people ate, there was a special dance performed around a kettle of dogmeat. After a few prayers, certain dancers danced around the kettle and then pretended to attack it, as if it were an enemy. At the conclusion of the dance, they speared the choicest parts of the dogmeat and presented them to the older men of the tribe. Then everyone participated in the feast prepared by the women.

Even though many of the symbolic aspects of the Grass dance have been forgotten, the dance is still performed by all Plains tribes. Even tribes from other areas join in. It is still called the Grass dance by many, but the most popular name today is War dance. Now, just as it was then, it has nothing to do with war. It is simply a social dance in which the dancers can once again imitate the old Indian way of life.

The War dance has been further popularized off the reservations by Indian show groups, which tour the country and perform at local tourist attractions. It is the dance most often seen at huge Indian celebrations and is usually held in conjunction with the Sun dance. In the wintertime, Indians often gather in indoor gymnasiums and recreation halls to dance the War dance far into the night.

Because the dance is appealing to the individual dancer, there have been a number of War dance styles to inundate the Northern Plains area. The fancy footwork of the Oklahoma Indians is popular to some degree on Northern reservations. The slower "old-time" style is still done by some of the ancient members of the tribes. One of the most popular styles in recent times to spread throughout the Northern Plains, as well as other parts of the country, is sometimes called the Northern style of War dancing. This style is particularly popular among the Mandan, Arikara, and Gros

Ventre, the Plains Cree and Ojibwa, and the Northern Sioux tribes. Its highest concentration is in the state of North Dakota.

The Northern style has certain features which make it outstanding even to the untrained eye. Its particular advocates are the younger generation of Indian dancers; the best are teen-agers. They wear costumes which are resplendent with heavily beaded cuffs, armbands, "suspenders" called harnesses, headbands, and other accessories. Shirts and trousers are covered with long, chainette fringe sewn in triangular or V-shaped designs, and long ribbons hang down from their back loincloths, or aprons. (Because of this, they are sometimes referred to as ribbon dancers.) Northern-style music is especially high-pitched, and a great number of renditions of each song are sung so that the dancers are on the floor for longer periods of time. Some dancers carry long whistles, which they blow over the heads of the singers, indicating that they want the singers to continue the song. The dance is often a test of endurance.

The footwork and body movements are spectacular. The dancers are lithe and supple; they have a relaxed and bouncy style somewhat resembling a puppet dancing on a string. They dart quickly, changing direction, now dropping close to the ground, then suddenly shooting upward to full height. Occasionally they shake their rumps or torsos in spastic quivers. Their footwork is masterful; sometimes they appear to stumble or limp, only to quickly recover in precise rhythm of the drum and song. Choreographically, the dance has great aesthetic value even to the non-Indian spectator.

Athletic dancing such as this lends itself very well

to competition. It is no wonder, then, that War dance contests are becoming very popular on the Northern reservations. Influenced by the white man and the Southern Plains tribes of Oklahoma, contests can be found on all reservations. Dancers often travel great distances to compete in reservation-wide or regional competitions. Trophies, ribbons, and cash prizes are awarded the winners. Smaller contests may pay only a few dollars; however, at some of the larger celebrations, first prize may be as much as $500.

As in other aspects of Indian society, music and dance have always been susceptible to change. The Indian has historically retained much of his Indianness but has added various white man's innovations to his own traditional culture. Music and dance are good examples.

Songs, for instance, which might have become obsolete once the Indians were placed on reservations, have had renewed vigor as a result of the World Wars, Korea, and Vietnam. The old war songs, which once celebrated the deeds of warrior fighting against hostile tribes, were reinstated to proclaim the valorous deeds of the Indian soldiers fighting against the enemies of the United States.

Here are some examples of songs translated from the Sioux:

World War I:
There's a fight over there
The Indian boys will go there
The Long Knives [United States Government]
    have said this

World War II:

Adolph Hitler, when you come charging, you
don't bring many men
You are weak!
"I took the German's land
I took the Japanese land and I made peace"
All over the world the soldiers are returning
saying this
Bad Moccasins [a man's name] said this:
"When the people come together, think of me
I like to have a good time [dance and sing]
but I'm in the Army now
The Germans have wounded me, and I am
        returning home with difficulty"
The flag of the United States is standing in Berlin
The Indian boys did this

Korea:

They are shooting as they charge
In Korea, they are shooting as they charge
The Indian boys carry the [sacred] pipe, shooting
        as they charge
In Korea they are shooting as they charge
They're charging over here
The Indian boys are charging
Overseas, the [North] Koreans are crying at last
They're charging over here
The Indian boys are charging

As of 1968, there were still no songs composed about
Vietnam, but more than likely the Indians will eventually get around to composing even more songs about

Indian heroes on foreign lands, as long as there are more battles to be fought.

The English language is frequently used in Indian song texts, often as a parody of the white man. The texts usually make the Indians laugh, not so much because the lyrics are humorous, but because the words are sung in a stereotyped manner, exactly how the white man would sing them in some crooning ballad.

A Round dance song from Pine Ridge:

Hello, honey, dearie
I would like to see you tonight
In the valley
In the valley of the moon

Another from North Dakota:

My darlin', I love you
Why can't I marry you?

When English lyrics are used they are always interspersed with vocables. Often the Indians mix English with their native language in the same song.

Again from the North Dakota Sioux:

Dearie, many a time I want to see you
Wanciyanka cana imasteca
[When I see you I'm bashful]

As is obvious the English lyrics are most often based on a love theme. One of the most popular songs heard all over the country is simply:

She got mad at me because I said hello to
my old-timer!

Not only has the traditional musical heritage of the
Plains Indian changed; it has been greatly augmented
by Euro-American musical forms. All kinds of non-
Indian music are firmly implanted on the reservations.
The Federal and mission schools teach a number of
instruments to the Indian children, and bands are as
important to their athletic events as they are to non-
Indian rallies. The Indians of this region have been
exposed particularly to Western and country music, and
many Indians have become proficient on the guitar and
play in Western bands. The transition to rock 'n' roll,
of course, has been inevitable, with the abundance of
radios and television sets. The young Indian teen-ager
who stomps it up in the War dances during the afternoon is very likely to be seen in the evening, frugging
and jerking with his best girl at the local "white" dance.
Teen-age dances are often held in conjunction with
traditional Indian powwows. While the Indian dances
are in progress under the brush arbors the all-Indian
rock bands are blaring from a nearby community hall.
The parents of the Indian teen-agers appear to be as
frustrated as their non-Indian counterparts, preferring
the pulsating throb of the drum and falsetto songs to
the amplified cacophony of the young people. Shaking
their heads at the long-haired boys and miniskirted girls,
they often voice the clichéd question of all ages: "What
is this younger generation coming to?"

9 Games and Sports

JUST AS music and dance served important functions in the everyday life of the Plains Indian, various kinds of games and sports provided a welcome relief from the rigors and hardships of camp life. Games not only provided activities for leisure time, but were instrumental in training young boys and girls in the roles they would play as adults.

Athletic events, on the other hand, served much the same purpose as warfare. Here was another opportunity in which a young brave could make a name for himself as an expert horseman or skillful marksman and at the same time keep himself fit for the battles that were to come. Foot racing and horse racing were both events which required endurance and a determination to win, both prerequisites for the adventurous warrior. Stickball games provided an arena in which the young men could display their stamina and courage. Often, men's societies competed with each other on the ball field, and many a bloody encounter ensued between the two in the heat of the game. Armed with playing sticks, the opposing teams often beat each other mercilessly in

183

Sees the Ground, Pretty Paint, Comes Up Red, and Victor Singer,
Crow Indians from Montana, lined up to begin a footrace.

the attempt to push the leather ball across the opponent's goal.

Another important aspect of the Plains Indian's personality was his insatiable desire to gamble. Just as he
threw himself recklessly into the pursuit of enemies,
he sometimes wagered all his possessions on the out-
come of a sporting event. All tribes had certain forms
of gambling known as hand games, stick games, or
moccasin games, depending on the tribe. These were
games of skill and chance in which individuals or teams
faced each other and tried to outguess the opposition.
In one form of the game, pebble, plumstone, or bullet

was hidden underneath one of several moccasins, and the opposition had to guess under which one it lay. The moccasin games were accompanied by frenetic singing and hand gesturing to confuse the guessing team. Scores were kept by wooden markers. The team that won all the markers won the game. Often, societies or entire communities would challenge each other, and the games would go on endlessly through the night.

A similar game played by the Sioux is called Hiding a Stick. The rules of the game were described in Frances Densmore's "Teton Sioux Music" by her interpreter, Robert P. Higheagle:

Ten people play on each side and 10 score sticks are used. One player from each side is chosen, these two competing to see which side shall first hide the stick. They sit on the ground opposite each other, and each has a little stick which he transfers rapidly from one hand to the other, his opponent watching and trying to determine which hand holds the stick. The player who conceals the stick most successfully thereby secures two score sticks for his side, in addition to the privilege of being the first side to hide the stick. The two lines of players are seated on the ground, and the leader of each side selects two players. These sit in front of the other players, facing each other, and each with a hiding-stick. The side whose representative won in the first contest is the side which first conceals the sticks, the opposing players being the guessers. If the location of one of the sticks is correctly guessed, the guessing side takes one score stick from the two acquired by their opponents in the first test. If the guessing side fails to

locate the second hiding-stick, the rules require that
the score stick be returned to the hiding side. If the
guessing side succeeds in locating the second hiding-
stick, they take the remaining score stick from the
other side. The score sticks are taken from the opponent's pile as long as he has any, after which they
are taken from the unappropriated pile on the
ground. The leader of either side may at any time
withdraw a player who is not successful and substitute one from the remaining players. The play of
each side continues until the opponents have guessed
the location of both sticks, and the game continues
until one side has won all the score sticks.

The following signals are used to indicate guesses:
Extending the first and second fingers and pointing
toward the right indicates a guess that both players
have the stick in their left hands. Similarly, pointing toward the left indicates a guess that both
players have the stick in their right hands. Extending
the right hand with the fingers spread means "the
players have the sticks in the *outside* hands." The
right arm descending with the hand cleaving the air
like a knife means "the players have the sticks in the
inside hands."

A war song was often sung at the conclusion of the
game by the victorious players, inserting an opponent's
name in the song in place of the enemy's.

A variation of the stick game was played by Assiniboine women, as well as women of other tribes. Forty-
one peeled sticks were used in the game. Individuals or
teams of women faced each other, as in the hiding the

stick game. One player took the forty-one sticks, placed them behind her back, and divided them into two piles. Then she held the two bundles in front of her, and the opponent tried to guess which hand held the even or odd sticks.

Girls and boys rarely played together. The young girls imitated their mothers and aunts, playing house and making small tipis and dolls, which they carried around in miniature cradles. Much of the young girl's time was spent helping her female relatives with the cooking and learning crafts that would make her eligible for marriage.

Likewise, boys imitated the actions of their male relatives. As soon as they were old enough to walk, their fathers or uncles taught them to shoot small bows and arrows and hunt for birds. The young boys concentrated on games which would sharpen their skills as hunters and warriors. They often imitated the chiefs or medicine men of the tribe, holding councils and pretending to cure people. It appears that "playing doctor" was not limited to non-Indian children. Often older boys put on Sun dances, piercing themselves through their buckskin shirts, rather than their flesh.

Many games were played for sheer amusement, and variations of games played today by non-Indian children, such as follow-the-leader, tag, and hide-and-seek, were popular. Games to make others laugh or to frighten them were also favorites. George Bushotter, a full-blooded Sioux who worked with the anthropologist, J. Owen Dorsey, told of the following "ghost" game played by boys and girls in an article published in *American Anthropologist* in 1891:

One erects a lodge at a distance from the village, and at night he comes hooting like an owl and scratching on the exterior of the tent, where other children are seated. Sometimes the ghost whistles just as they imagine that ghosts do. Some ghosts whiten their faces and paint their bodies at random. Others put red paint around their eyes. All this is at night when their mothers are absent. Occasionally the children leave the village in order to play this game, going in a crowd to the designated place. Some ghosts whiten their bodies all over, painting themselves black between the ribs. When they do not whiten the whole face they cover the head with white paper, in which they punch eyeholes, around which they make black rings. The one acting the ghost tickles anyone whom he catches until the latter laughs very heartily.

Since the Northern Plains enjoys four distinct seasons, many of the games played by children and young adults were determined by the time of year. There appears to be a great similarity of seasonal games not only throughout the Northern Plains, but the rest of North America as well. This suggests that not only material culture, music and dance, and arts and crafts diffused readily through most of the country, but that the same was true of games.

In the wintertime, boys slid down slopes on sleds made of the rib cages of buffalo. A special game, sometimes called snowsnake, was played on long, narrow, icy runways. A stick carved to represent a snake was hurled down the icy lane, each boy trying to make his stick go farther than the others. The same game was played with a buffalo or cow horn, into which was inserted a wooden shaft tipped with a feather. The horn was thrown along the ice in the same manner as the snow snake.

In the spring the boys enjoyed mud fights. They packed mud balls around willow sticks and flung them at their opponents. Hoop-and-javelin was also a favorite game. A hoop was fashioned from willow and rawhide and constructed in such a way that the rawhide thongs bisected the hoop to form a net. A spear, or javelin, was thrown at the rolling hoop, and points were scored on the basis of what netted section of the hoop was speared.

Bushotter reports a variation of this game for the Sioux:

> The men hunt the deer, and when they return to camp the boys take part of the hides and cut them into narrow strips, which they soak in water; they make a hoop of ash wood, all over which they put the strips of raw hide, which they interweave in such a way as to leave a hole in the middle, which they call the "heart." The players form two sides of equal number, and ti-oshpaye or gens usually plays against gens. The hoop is thrown by one of the players toward those on the other side. They are provided with sharp-pointed sticks, each of which is forked at the small end. As the hoops roll they throw at it, in order to thrust one of the sticks through the heart. When one hits the heart he keeps the hoop for his side, and he and his comrades chase their opponents,

who flee with their blankets spread out behind them in order to deaden the force of any blow from a pursuer. When the pursuer overtakes one of the fugitives they strike him with the hoop as hard as they can; then they abandon the pursuit and return to their former place, while the one hit with the hoop takes it and shows it, making it roll towards the players on the other side. As it rolls he says to them, "Ho, there is a buffalo returning to you." When the stick does not fall out of the heart, they say that the hoop belongs to the player who threw the stick. This is not a game of chance but of skill, which has been played by large boys since the olden times.

Many other nonseasonal games were reminiscent of boys of other lands: swinging from ropes in trees, climbing and jumping from high places on a dare, spinning tops, and shooting at targets with willow spears.

When Indians were placed under Federal jurisdiction and it became mandatory for Indian children to attend government or missionary schools, they adapted easily to the new games and sports of the white man. While Plains Indians have never lost their love of horses and horse racing, most of the other traditional games have become obsolete. In their place the Indians pursue baseball, football, basketball, and other varsity sports.

Over the years there has been more interest in basketball and track than in any other sports. The reason for this is probably that in the early years of formal schooling on the reservations, football and baseball equipment was too expensive for the schools to buy.

Basketball requires only a ball and two hoops, and track equipment is easily improvised.

Basketball games are played intramurally between schools on the same reservation, as well as against all-white teams from bordering communities. Intertribal games are also popular. One of the best known is the Tournament of Tribal Champions played last year in Brigham City, Utah. Sixteen tribes participated, including some from Montana, Wyoming, Nevada, and the Dakotas.

Despite basketball's un-Indianness, each game is more than likely to retain certain tribal characteristics. This can be a great disadvantage to non-Indian teams or teams from a different tribe. Under the pressure of the game, commands for offensive and defensive plays are often shouted across the floor to teammates in the native language, much to the bewilderment of the opponents. The Indian players can talk about their strategy freely as the game is in progress, without their opposition being the wiser.

Like any other game, basketball has its followers and fans. All-Indian bands play at quarter and half time, and young, bouncy cheerleaders lead their teams' supporters in victory chants. Some of the cheers are in the native language also, like the following from the Holy Rosary Mission school on the Pine Ridge Sioux Reservation:

Ohiya, Ohiya, Ohiya po!
Rosary, Rosary, *Iya po!*
Hiyu po, hiyu po, luzahan

Will we win now? *Han, Han, Han!*
(Win, Win, Win!
Rosary, Rosary, go!
Come on, come on, quickly
Will we win now? Yes, Yes, Yes!)

Tempsilala, tempsilala, sha, sha, sha!
Shred 'em up, shred 'em up, Rah! Rah! Rah!
Tapalala, tapalala, icu po!
Rosary, Rosary, *iya po!*
(Turnips, turnips, red, red, red!
Shred 'em up, shred 'em up, Rah! Rah! Rah!
Rosary, Rosary, go!)
[Red turnip is actually the Sioux word for carrot;
tapalala is the traditional word for ball.]

The Oglala Sioux made world history in track events
when one of their sons, Billy Mills, became the first
American to win the gold medal for the 10,000-meter
race at the 1964 Olympics in Tokyo. He was also presented the Gustavius T. Kirby Award for "exemplary
sportsmanship by a member of the United States Olympic team" by the Sportsmanship Brotherhood. The
award was presented to him at a dinner at the Hotel
Americana in New York City on January 14, 1965. The
room was crowded with sportswriters and well-known
athletes. The award was made by Jay-Ehret Mahoney, a
prominent New York attorney and past president of the
Amateur Athletic Union. Mahoney said of Mills: "From
a land of rock and sand that no white man considered
worth taking from the Indian, there comes to us this
new symbol to take his place with Longboat, Tawa-

(Bob Mathews)

Billy Mills, Oglala Sioux from Pine Ridge, South Dakota, the first American to win the 10,000-meter race in the Olympic games. He is shown here with Jay-Ehret Mahoney, past president of the Amateur Athletic Union, when he was awarded a plaque from the Sportsmanship Brotherhood.

nima, and Thorpe, to show all of us this new conscience, this new awareness that there is a place in this man's world for each and every one of us."

Mahoney also called the young Sioux athlete "a symbol of confidence and achievement to the American Indian." When Mahoney concluded his speech, a group of young Indians stood and sang an honor song for their new hero. Even at the Hotel Americana, Indian tradition has its place.

Mills accepted the award and replied with typical Indian humor; "I recently met Roger Maris, and find we have something in common. He makes one-hundred-thousand dollars a year, and I run one-hundred-thous-and miles a year."

At the conclusion of the ceremony, Enos Poor Bear, then chairman of the Oglala Sioux Tribal Council, presented Mills with a check for $1,000, a war-bonnet, pair of beaded moccasins, and the new Indian name, Makoce Tehila, or Loves Country. The Indian ceremony was no different than it would have been 1,700 miles away on the Pine Ridge Reservation.

In the summertime, baseball and softball are popular on the reservations. Most communities have their own ball diamond, and teams are sponsored by the local schools, American Legion posts, or other organizations, much the same as in white communities. The competitive spirit always prevails, and it is frequent to hear the master of ceremonies of an Indian powwow interrupt the singing and dancing to announce the afternoon ball scores. In very recent years, swimming pools have been built on some reservations, and it would appear that in the near future, swimming may become a competitive summertime sport.

Probably the most important spectator sport of all Northern Plains reservations is the rodeo. With their natural affinity for horses and high value on horseman-ship, it is no wonder that many of the young Indian boys aspire to become champion rodeo riders and per-formers. Just as the conservative Indian men can

(Courtesy John Colhoff)

Indian bronco rider at a rodeo.

organize a powwow overnight, the young Indian bucks can instigate a small rodeo with a few head of stock, a dilapidated snow fence for a coral, and a few reckless riders ready to earn a name for themselves. Again, the ingredients are there: daring, competition, and fame.

While there are hundreds of smaller rodeos going on all summer long in the reservation communities, many of the larger ones have become established throughout the years. The rodeos, which have earned a reputation for having challenging stock, as well as top cash prizes, are the Crow Indian Fair and Rodeo, held near Crow Agency, Montana, in mid-August; The Wolf Point Wild Horse Stampede on the Fort Peck Reservation in July; The Arapaho Indian Fair and Rodeo at Ethete, Wyoming; and the Rosebud Indian Fair held in late August in South Dakota.

Indian riders also participate in the famous Cheyenne Frontier Days, the Calgary Stampede in Canada, and some travel to the Pendleton Roundup in Oregon. In several western states, there are all-Indian rodeos sponsored by various tribal groups.

Many small rodeos are held in conjunction with community fairs and powwows. I attended one in the summer of 1967 at Parmelee, South Dakota, on the Rosebud Reservation, which was held concurrent with the community's annual powwow.

The corral was fashioned from a heavy-duty wire fence, around which the spectators parked their cars. In the old days, I recalled, a simple snow fence was used. The spectators parked their cars around the perimeter of the corral, not only because they had a vantage point of seeing all the action, but because they could also discourage a wild horse or bull from charging through the shabby fence by blowing their horns and frightening the animal away. Today the auto horn is blown as applause for a cowboy who stays on his bucking horse for the required time.

The cowboys waited by the chutes for their turn to ride. Young boys and girls mounted on spirited horses encircled the cars looking for friends. Some walked

Clowns try to distract the bull from trampling its Indian rider at a rodeo.

their mounts, others rode at breakneck speed around the spectators. Occasionally we could hear the songs still being sung at the dance arbor a few hundred yards away.

"Comin' outta chute Number Three," the announcer bellowed over the public address system. The chute gate opened, and a lean youth atop a belligerent mare bucked into the arena. Dust rose, and the horse snorted fiercely as it tried to shake its rider. Suddenly the rider and horse separated, going separate ways, the rider hitting hard against the ground. Two pick-up men rode around the horse, forcing it away from the unprotected rider, and chased it to the opposite end of the corral into another pen. The rider limped back to the chute, dusting off his chaps with his hat.

"Let's give 'im a hand," the announcer said. He was met with a series of blasts from the auto horns.

The next rider fared no better. He was immediately smashed against the side of the chute as his horse bucked out. About three jumps later, he was sitting on the ground with a glazed look in his eyes. The horse bucked merrily along one side of the fence until it reached the pen.

The third rider was a real professional. His horse came out of the chutes balking, but soon it was twisting and turning high in the air. The rider, clenching to his loose rope around the horse's stomach with one hand, and cleaving the air with the other, met each buck with ease. A whistle blew, indicating that the rider had stayed on the full ten seconds, and the spectators blared their auto horns loudly.

Interspersed between bareback and saddle bronco riding, there were other events, such as calf roping and bulldogging. Agile riders dropped from their fast-paced horses, grabbing onto the horns of the steer and wrestling it to the ground. Two-man teams chased mischievous calves around the arena until one caught its neck with a lariat and the other its hind legs. Time was important. The rider who could accomplish his feats of skill in less time than the others was the winner.

The rodeo continued all afternoon until it was time for the evening meal. Later that night the tough cowboys strutted around the powwow grounds listening to one another brag of their warriorlike prowess in the rodeo arena. Some would try for the big money in the national rodeos. Others would go to Hollywood, where they might be hired to "play" Indian, riding and taking falls in the latest Western movie.

10 Language

IF YOU were to travel across the Great Plains in the early days, you would have found that most tribes could not converse with one another. While the various bands of Teton, Santee, and Yankton Sioux could readily understand one another, their dialects were different. They were unable to understand their best allies, the Cheyenne and Arapaho, and had to resort to translations by a very few people who spoke more than one language. In many cases, tribes meeting on friendly terms to trade had to resort to sign language.

Anthropologists and linguists discovered that the languages of some tribes were similar. After studying these languages, they divided them into linguistic families, or language stocks. Languages, though not mutually intelligible by the tribes that spoke them, were classified together on the basis of similar root words. Thus, the Dakota and their mortal enemies, the Crow, were classified under the same stock because of speech similarities, yet they could not understand each other. Their languages simply shared a common origin.

The largest language stock was the Algonkian, which

included many tribes of the Eastern Woodlands. On the Plains, the Algonkian speakers were represented by the Cheyenne, Arapaho, Gros Ventre, Blackfeet, Piegan, Blood, Plains Ojibwa, and Plains Cree. Their languages were related to the Sac and Fox, Menomini, Potawatomi, Delaware, and other tribes which lived to the east of them. Longfellow used an abundance of Algonkian words in his *Song of Hiawatha*.

The next largest language stock was the Siouan. It received its name from the largest tribe on the Plains, the Sioux. The Sioux had four dialects: Teton, Yankton, Santee, and Assiniboine. The other tribes of this stock were divided into the Upper Missouri, which included the Crow, Hidatsa, and Mandan; and the Lower Missouri, consisting of the Iowa, Kansa, Missouri, Omaha, Osage, Oto, and Ponca. Also in this stock were the Quapaw and Winnebago.

Many of our Midwestern states were named after tribes of the Siouan stock, including Minnesota, a Siouan term meaning smoky water, and Nebraska, a southern Siouan word meaning trampled flat. The Santee Sioux called themselves Dakota; hence, North and South Dakota. Iowa means sleepy.

In the Caddoan stock, named after one of its principal tribes, the Caddo, we find the great Pawnee Republic in Nebraska, and the Arikara of North Dakota. The Sarsi were members of the Athabascan stock.

Indian languages have often been portrayed in movies and on television as being very simple in structure and limited in use. However, most languages were complicated. Some tribes had vocabularies of 30,000 words. The average English speaker has a vocabulary of 10,000, and rarely uses more than 900 words in everyday speech.

The common concept that all Indians say "How" comes from the Plains Indians. Most of them used "How" (usually written "Hau"), or a variation such as "Ho," "Haw," or a nasal "Hahn," as a greeting similar to "Hello." It was also used as an expression of approval, generally translated "good." The Indian speaker sometimes shortened "Hau" to "Hmm." This peculiarity led later writers to use the cliched word, "Ugh!"—a word never heard on the Plains or anywhere else.

Many Indian languages would be easier for Europeans or Asians than for white Americans to learn. The sentence structure of many Indian languages is similar to Japanese, French, or German. Many Plains languages, for instance, reverse the order of words in their sentences. Instead of saying "I am going to the dance," a Sioux would say, "Dance to the I am going." Like Japanese, there are some languages which have "spoken" question marks and periods. In Sioux, *"Blo pahi* yelo" means "He is picking potatoes." *Blo pahi* he?" means, "Is he picking potatoes?" The two sentences are the same except for the last word, which indicates that the sentence is either declarative or interrogative.

Indian languages are replete with nasal (like French) and gutteral (like German) sounds. Some are harsh languages, some very soft. In most tribes men and women speak differently. A Sioux man would say, *"Hiyu* wo!" "Come here!" A woman would say, *"Hiyu* we!" the last syllable being different. If a man were to say, *"Hiyu* we," it would mean "Please come here." Among some tribes, men and women used different interjections. In short, a man and woman being hit with a stick would have different ways of saying Ouch!

When the Europeans appeared, first with the horse and gun, then liquor, beads, cloth, and other commercially manufactured trade goods, the Indians had to invent words for these things. The Indians' language was very picturesque in its descriptions of foreign materials.

Preceding the appearance of the white man on the Plains, was the horse. The Sioux, never having seen one before, called it *sunka wakan,* or mysterious dog. A whole series of new words had to be developed with the arrival of the horse—words for saddle, bridle, stirrups, tether, hobble, halter, bit, and martingale. Since the horse was truly "mysterious," there were ceremonies performed in its honor, and new customs developed with regard to raising, training, and even capturing it. One horse probably forced each Indian tribe to add hundreds of new words and concepts to its vocabulary.

The railroad was called *maza canku,* or "iron road" and the steamboat, *peta weta,* "fire boat." The Sioux called the wagons in which the early settlers arrived *canpagmiyanpi* or "it goes on around things made of wood." When the first wireless poles were strung along the Prairie, they called this strange phenomenon, *wikancala woglaka,* or "talking wires," a term which was later to describe the radio. A telephone was called *mas' waape,* or "striking metal," indicating the bell clapper. When the Sioux saw the first automobile, they called it *iyecinkala inyanke,* or "it runs by itself," much as the white man called it horseless carriage. Airplanes were called *kinye kinyanpi* or "they fly above."

As the Sioux met foreigners they invented words for the newcomers. The Siouan word for white man is *wasicun*. Little is known about the origin of this word. The root *sicun* is one of four Sioux words for soul, or spirit, and it is likely that the first Indians to see a white man may have considered him a kind of spirit. There is another story about the origin which the Sioux remember today. They say that a long time ago, they saw the first white trapper in Indian land. The trapper came to an Indian village to trade. He finished his business and, upon leaving camp, noticed some fat hanging on a wooden frame. Fat in Siouan is called *wasin*. The Indians say that the white man was so hungry that he took some pieces of fat to eat. Some of the women saw him and cried out, *"Wasin icu!"* ("He took the fat!") The next time the Indians saw a white man, they recalled the incident and said of the stranger, "There goes another fat taker!" The words *wasin icu* were later contracted into *wasicun*. While the story seems somewhat contrived, it is considered by some Indians to be the authentic genesis of their term for white man.

The Sioux called the first missionaries (Catholic) *sina sapa,* usually translated black robe. They later called the Catholic Church *sapa un,* or "they wear black," to differentiate them from the Episcopalians, whom they called *ska un,* or "they wear white."

The Sioux saw their first Negro soldiers and called them *ha sapa,* meaning black-skinned. Chinese and Italian immigrants worked on the railroads that cut through the Sioux country. These Chinese were known as *pecoka hanska,* a word which refers to the long queue of the Chinese worker's hairstyle. The Sioux watched the Italians measuring the distance between railroad ties by the length of their feet and appropriately called them *si hanska* or "big feet." The Sioux, upon meeting the first Jews, thought they resembled the Italians and erroneously called them big feet also. Most Sioux today have forgotten the original group for whom the word was intended, and *si hanska* is the current word for Jew.

The Sioux called the United States Government *mila hanska,* or "long knives" (swords), and later *tunka-silayapi,* which means "they have him for a grand-father." During World Wars I and II the Sioux called the Germans *iya sica, or* "bad talkers," and the Japa-nese *pecoka hanska* (the same word for Chinese) or *kisunla,* which means "braided down the middle," an-other reference to the queue.

As more and more white men came into the Indian territory, English became a lingua franca of the Plains. The younger generation of Sioux speakers slowly began to replace many of the old words with English substi-tutes. After all, it was easier to say car than *iyecinkala inyanke. Mazaskanskan tonakca hwo?* became "Time" *tona he?* (What time is it?) Today most Indian lan-guages include both English and native Indian words; generally, the nouns, especially names of recently in-troduced items, are spoken in English, while the rest of the sentence conforms to traditional Indian grammar.

Most of the traders who set up posts along the rivers and near the forts were able to speak a little Indian, but few could do more than say a few common ex-pressions, know the names of the commodities in which they dealt, and count money or pelts. Many of the traders took Indian wives. Their children were usually able to speak both languages fluently but were notoriously bad interpreters. In fact, history shows that many of the animosities between Indians and whites were caused by misinterpretations at treaties and councils.

Indian languages were not written before the white man arrived. Some of the early explorers and journalists made word lists of the strange new languages, but it was not until the missionaries arrived that entire alphabets were developed for the Indian tongues. The Jesuits were the most notable philologists. It was their policy to learn the language of the new people and then translate the sermons and later the Bible, prayer books, and hymns into the native dialects.

Following is a literal translation of the Lord's Prayer translated into the Lakota dialect of Sioux by the Jesuit, Reverend Eugene Buechel:

Ateunyanpi, mahpiya ekta nanke cin, nicaje wakanlapi ni;

> Our Father, heaven in You are, Your name may they consider holy;

nitokiconze u ni;

> may Your kingdom come;

mahpiya ekta tokel nitawacin econpi kin he iyecel maka akanl econpi ni.

> heaven in how Your will they do the that in the same manner earth on may they do it.

Aneptu kin otoiyohi aguyapi kin anpetu kin le el unk'upi ye;

> Day the each bread the day the this on give us;

na waunhtanipi kin unkakiciktonjapi ye,

> and we sin the they forgive us,

*unkis tona sicaya ecaunkiconpi kin iyecel awicaun-
kiciktonjapi;*
we how badly they do to us the in the same manner
we forgive them;
na taku wawiyutan un kin el
and something to be tried on account of the toward
*unkayapi sni ye, tka taku sice kin etanhan eungla-
kupi ye.*
take us not but something bad the from take us
back again. Amen.

Anthropologists developed what is known as the International Phonetic System, a series of characters,
most of which were variations of the Roman and
Greek alphabets, which could be used to write the
sounds of any language in the world. Later this alphabet
was refined into phonemic alphabets. A phonemic alphabet has only one sound for one character—unlike
French and English, but much like Spanish.

Today, many of the languages of larger tribes are
written and have published dictionaries and grammars.
At one time a newspaper was published in the Santee
dialect. Frequently, signs on reservations are written
in Indian, and in some cities where there are large Indian populations, radio broadcasts are made in native languages. The United States Government publishes a
series of readers in native languages and English called
bilingual readers, for the purpose of teaching young
Indians their native languages. Today, more than sixty
percent of all Indians in the United States and Canada
speak their native tongue as a first language and have
to learn English before going to school.

11 Famous Men and Battles

I N PRE-COLUMBIAN times, literally thousands of battles were fought on the Northern Plains, ranging from small forays involving only a handful of warriors to massive movements of entire villages against their traditional enemies. The names of great leaders of these expeditions, as well as the battles themselves, were often recorded in the winter counts or handed down verbally for generations. With the passing of time, many of the war stories were forgotten or replaced by more significant ones.

The best documented accounts of Indian warfare are concerned with the battles fought between the Indians and the United States Government. Volumes of books have been written from both the white man's and the Indian's point of view. The fighting techniques employed in these battles are still used in some military academies to teach strategy. Yet to the majority of people, these episodes in American history are little known.

The Northern Plains was the last stronghold of what

The Oglala chief, Red Cloud, the only Indian to win a war from the United States. This photo was taken in 1872, probably by Alexander Gardner, shortly after the end of the Red Cloud War.

the government called Indian hostility. Most of the battles were fought in the 1860's and 1870's. The Civil War had ended, and many of the United States military leaders were sent West to fight Indians. By this time, most of the tribes had signed treaties with the United States, and reservation life was imminent.

Battles between the United States and the Northern Plains tribes were fought over and over for the same reasons: encroaching whites, broken treaties. Wagon roads and railroads cut through Indian-owned land, bringing white men hungry for adventure. Gold and other minerals were discovered, thus encouraging even more white men from the great Eastern cities to come to the new land of promise. Forts were established; buffalo were slaughtered; the Indians were forced onto reservations. Indeed, these were good reasons to make the Plains Indians hostile.

In American history books, the battles won by the United States are often referred to as skirmishes, wars, or defensive maneuvers. The battles won by the Indians are invariably labeled massacres. The student interested in discovering for himself the real causes and effects of these battles is invited to read some of the accounts listed in the bibliography. However, no book on the Northern Plains would be complete without briefly mentioning two controversial encounters between the United States and Indians. Traditionally, one has been called a battle, the other a massacre, giving some indication of who won each. A word about the great men who led their people in these encounters, as well as about the battles themselves, is necessary in order to understand the events which led to the final resistance by the Indians and their ultimate defeat.

The first battle is probably the best known and the least understood of all. It is usually called the Little Big Horn Massacre, or Custer's Last Stand. The events which led to the Custer incident are worth considering.

In 1865 the United States Government proposed that a series of forts be built along the Bozeman Trail, which cut across Wyoming and Montana and was a favorite hunting ground of the Sioux, Cheyenne, and Arapaho.

One who voiced great opposition to this proposal was Red Cloud, a feared warrior of the Oglala Sioux, who had proved his prowess against tribal enemies as a young man. At age forty-four, Red Cloud was determined to prevent the hordes of white emigrants from encroaching any farther. With a party of Sioux and Cheyenne, he intercepted the first pary of construction workers and kept them at gunpoint for two weeks.

The government tried to negotiate, but Red Cloud refused to allow safe passage. Despite his threats, the government began building the forts, the largest of which was Fort Phil Kearney. Red Cloud took to the warpath and harassed all white men along the Bozeman Trail for two years. His defiant campaign was called the Red Cloud War.

In December, 1866, the soldiers were to feel the wrath of Red Cloud. A group of workers left Fort Phil Kearney to cut timber in a nearby stand. They were surrounded by Red Cloud's warriors, who kept them under siege for most of the day. Captain William J. Fetterman and 80 men were sent to rescue the party. Although given orders not to pursue the Indians, Fetterman disobeyed and was led by a wily Sioux decoy into ambush. He and his total command were encircled and annihilated. This episode in the Red Cloud War was known as the Fetterman Massacre.

A close contemporary of Red Cloud, a great warrior and religious leader of the Hunkpapa Sioux, called it by a different name. He had a vision before the Fetterman battle in which he saw Sioux warriors killing 100 white men. He called it the Battle of the Hundred Slain. His name was Sitting Bull.

Sitting Bull was to become the new champion of the Sioux cause. The Red Cloud War ended in 1868 with the signing of the Fort Laramie treaty. But it was not defeat which brought Red Cloud to the negotiation table. He signed the treaty only after Fort Phil Kearney was burned. He emerged from battle as the only Indian ever to win a war against the United States Government.

But Sitting Bull would not retire. Although the Fort Laramie treaty established the Great Sioux Reservation, Sitting Bull and his followers continued to hunt buffalo and war against traditional enemies and white men off the reservation. He was joined by a faction of Oglala under the leadership of another famous warior, Crazy Horse, who had become disenchanted with Red Cloud's treaty. Crazy Horse, a much younger man, hated the white men and all Indians who had "touched the pen."He preferred to hunt buffalo, rather than take handouts from the white men on the reservation. He would not become one of the Indians who gave up their traditional ways to hang around the forts and beg for food and liquor.

Crazy Horse was much younger than Red Cloud and Sitting Bull. He had been born in what is now South Dakota, the son of an Oglala religious man. His mother was the sister of the Sicangu chief, Spotted Tail. All his young life he had heard his people talk about their hatred for the white man. As he grew older he vowed not to acquiesce to the demands of the United States Government. He was destined first to taste victory, then end his life abruptly as a martyr of the Sioux people.

In 1874 there were rumors that gold had been discovered in the Black Hills, the sacred grounds of the Sioux. According to the Fort Laramie treaty, no white man was to trespass into Indian territory. A scientific expedition was sent to the Black Hills to confirm the rumor. As its military escort there rode a detachment of cavalry under the command of General George Armstrong Custer.

Custer was by this time a famous cavalry officer. He had made his name as the youngest officer in the United States Cavalry to attain the rank of general. Born in Ohio and raised in Michigan, he was graduated from the United States Military Academy at West Point and entered the Second United States Cavalry at the outbreak of the Civil War. He received a number of battlefield promotions throughout the battles of Manassas, Gettysburg, Yellow Tavern, and Fishers Hill. By the time he was twenty-three, he was a full-fledged general in the Union Army. When the Civil War ended, he elected to go West and fight Indians. Many of his faithful followers chose to follow their boy general, as he was called, to the Western frontier.

Although Custer was a brilliant strategist, he was also a nonconformist with an egotistical streak. He designed his own uniform, preferring a sailor blouse, red neckerchief, and buckskin trousers to the official uniform. He let his blond hair grow long, which caused the Indians to call him Long Hair. He also became well-known in Washington circles. Because of his strong individualism and political dealings, he soon fell into disfavor with President Ulysses S. Grant and was eventually broken in rank. But this did not deter Custer. He thought that with the right kind of publicity about his Indian campaigns, he might very well be considered for the Presidency in the next election. He soon had his opportunity to prove his strength against the renegade Indians.

The 1874 expedition confirmed the rumor. There was indeed gold in the Black Hills. Soon the country was being overrun by white men from the East, bent on making their fortunes in the South Dakota gold mines. Fearing more hostility from Sitting Bull, Crazy Horse, and other Indian leaders, the United States issued an order in December, 1875, directing all Indians to return to the reservations. Those Indians who did not return by January, 1876, would be deemed hostiles.

The severe winter made it difficult to travel the long distance back to the reservations, so some did not comply with the order. Many Sioux who had traveled a long way from their agency never received the message.

A massive campaign was organized against the Sioux. In charge was General Phil Sheridan, a veteran Indian fighter. Under him were Generals Alfred Terry, John Gibbon, and George Crook, who planned to entrap the hostile Sioux in a three-pronged attack.

Bad weather prevented all but Crook from marching on the Indians. He, along with General Joseph Reynolds, started in March in below zero weather. On March 17 they stumbled upon Crazy Horse's camp on the Powder River and took it by surprise, scattering the Indians' horses. In an amazing recovery, Crazy Horse led his warriors in a counterattack, beating off the cavalry.

Terry and his command finally left Fort Lincoln, Nebraska, on May 17, 1876. Riding with Terry's infantrymen was the U. S. Seventh Cavalry under the command of George Armstrong Custer. By the time

(Courtesy Plume Trading and Sales Company)
The great Hunkpapa warrior and religious
leader, Sitting Bull. This F. B. Fiske photo is
one of many taken of the old chief. He and
the Oglala, Crazy Horse, led the Sioux and
Cheyenne to victory over Custer.

they reached the Indian camp, however, Crook had
already suffered another terrible defeat at the hands
of Crazy Horse at the Battle of the Rosebud.

Terry set up a base camp at the confluence of the
Yellowstone and Powder Rivers. Major Marcus A.
Reno, with a portion of Custer's Seventh, was sent to
scout the Indians' trail. He discovered evidence that a
large body of Indians was moving to the vicinity of
the Little Big Horn River. Terry assigned Custer to
start out for the point where Reno had found the Indian

signs. He was to be joined by Gibbon, and the two forces would crush the Indian camp. So on June 24 Custer, accompanied by Major Reno and twelve companies of cavalry, began the march.

Indeed, the Indians were camped on the Little Big Horn. After Crook's defeat, Crazy Horse and Sitting Bull, along with other Sioux and Cheyenne bands, converged in the Big Horn Valley, where an immense camp was pitched. There were Oglala, Hunkpapa, Mniconjou, San Arc, Sicangu, and Cheyennes, numbering possibly 12,000 to 15,000 Indians. In addition to Crazy Horse and Sitting Bull, there were other noteworthy chiefs and warriors: Dull Knife, Two Moons, and Little Wolf of the Cheyenne and Rain-in-the-Face, Gall, and American Horse of the Sioux. The camps were pitched in a line along the Big Horn River.

Custer crossed the Big Horn divide on June 25, when his trail was discovered by two young Sioux boys. One of the boys was shot, but the other managed to escape and carry the news of the soldiers' presence back to his village. Custer had to make a quick decision. Despite his orders to wait for Gibbons, he decided to act immediately. He divided his command into three detachments (four if you count Captain McDougall's company, which carried the ammunition separately). Major Reno with three companies was told to ride straight into the village. Major Frederick Benteen and three companies were to attack the southern side. Custer would attack from the north with five companies. The companies were accompanied by Crow and Arikara scouts, hated enemies of the Sioux and Cheyenne.

Just what went through Custer's mind that day is a matter of conjecture. But surely he was confident of victory. This was exactly the kind of coup he needed to attain even more fame back in the East. So sure was he of his ability to "ride down the Sioux nation with a handful of men" that he reportedly said upon seeing the village, "Custer's luck. We've got them this time!"

Reno reached the Indians first. He was quickly repelled by the overwhelming odds and was forced to retreat to some nearby bluffs. Benteen met no Indians, but soon he was encountered by a messenger from Custer, who hastily rode up to him bearing the now classic message: "Benteen. Come on. Big Village. Bring packs. P.S. Bring packs."

But Custer could not be found. Preoccupied with their own fate, Reno's troops continued to fight off the swelling hordes led by Crazy Horse and Sitting Bull until suddenly the attack on his position abruptly stopped and the Indians rode off.

The reason they left Reno on the bluffs was that Custer at last had reached the Indian camp. Seeing some of the women and old men retreating ahead of him, he encouraged his warriors to charge. Four brave Cheyenne faced Custer's detachment and were killed in order to give the people a chance to escape. The slight detainment of Custer also gave Crazy Horse and his men the chance to leave Reno's position and muster for an attack on Long Hair. Confronted by the swirling mass of warriors, Custer commanded his men to head for a rising knoll, which would give them a vantage point. But Custer never made it to the top. Shooting their own horses to form breastworks, his men fought bitterly against the odds. In less than an hour, Custer and his entire command had been wiped out.

The Sioux were frantic over their victory. The bodies of the soldiers were stripped of clothing and valuables, scalped, and mutilated. All but Custer. He who had shorn his hair for the battle remained untouched, unscalped, with two bullet wounds, either of which might have been the fatal one. The white bodies lay strewn about the prairie in a thin line stretching almost to the crest of the knoll, demarking their vain efforts to reach the top.

Leaving Custer, the Sioux returned to fight Reno on the bluffs, where they killed 18 and wounded 43 before nightfall. The next morning the battle raged again. But the Indians grew tired of the fighting and broke camp that evening. All told, Reno had lost 57 men; 52 were wounded. The next day Generals Gibbon and Terry arrived to find the dead bodies of 208 men of the Seventh. Some of the bodies were never recovered. The sole survivor of Custer's detachment was a horse named Comanche.

The news, first published by the Bozeman *Times* on July 3, shocked the nation: "General Custer and 15 officers and EVERY MAN BELONGING TO THE FIVE COMPANIES WAS KILLED." The Indians had won the greatest victory of any war fought on the Northern Plains.

Custer was dead, but the Indians knew that more soldiers would come. For the next several months the Sioux and Cheyenne were constantly harassed by government troops under the command of Colonel Nelson A. Miles. Sitting Bull and some of his followers escaped to Canada, where they were given refuge by the Canadian Government as long as they did not cross the international border to fight the Americans.

(Courtesy Nebraska State Historical Society)
Gathering up the dead after the Wounded Knee Massacre. The frozen bodies of the dead were dumped onto wagons and hauled to their final resting place atop a peaceful knoll. Photo by G.E. Trager.

Crazy Horse did not flee with Sitting Bull. He was determined to stay in the country of his forefathers. In January, 1877, he was surprised by Miles, and his band was scattered. After a number of pleas from his tribesmen, he finally consented to surrender to the United States, rather than have his people face starvation on the Plains. So on May 6, 1877, Crazy Horse and his band of nearly 900 people surrendered at Fort Robinson, Nebraska. They were required to hand over their guns, ammunition, and more than 2,000 horses to the commandant.

Reservation life fared well for Crazy Horse in the beginning, but he soon became restless. He had earned a great reputation as a warrior and leader of his people and still commanded great respect from the reservation Indians. Some of the chiefs who had signed the treaties became jealous of his popularity and conspired against him. Even though Crazy Horse made it known that he would serve as a scout for the United States in their campaign against the Nez Perce, the conspiring chiefs spread the rumor that Crazy Horse was plotting to assassinate the commandant of the fort. When brought in for questioning, Crazy Horse saw that he was being led to the guardhouse. He quickly drew a knife from beneath his blanket and tried to fight his way out. A friend, Little Big Man, tried to stop the ensuing battle; Crazy Horse was stabbed in the back by a guard. Hours later he died in his parents' tipi. Fearing desecration of his body, his parents and other relatives sneaked away into the night and buried his body somewhere on the prairie. The exact spot was never revealed. Thus, Crazy Horse, at thirty-three years of age, who had faced danger against the enemy since an early age, died an unglorious death at the hands of the white man.

Sitting Bull fared no better. The Canadian Government refused him a reservation. Faced with starvation, the once mighty leader of his people was forced to surrender at Fort Buford, Montana, on July 19, 1881. He served as a prisoner of war for two years and then was permitted to live peacefully on the Standing Rock Reservation.

With the death of Crazy Horse and the surrender of Sitting Bull, the hope of the Sioux and Cheyenne faded. As a final insult, the United States Government in 1886 issued an order prohibiting the Plains Indians to participate in their annual Sun dances, claiming that the ceremony was built on pagan beliefs and heinous torture. The Indian would now be forced to abandon his traditional ways and begin his trek along the white man's road to civilization.

This chain of events might well have marked the final chapter in the history of the Plains Indian. The struggle had ended; the wars were a glorious memory of the recent past. But one more episode was taking form. East of the Plains, a Paiute Indian living in Nevada had a new hope for the Indians of the Northern Plains.

His name was Wovoka. In 1888, during a total eclipse of the sun, he had a revelation which predicted that the old Indians who had died, as well as the buffalo, would return to the earth, and the white man would perish in a forthcoming cataclysmic event.

Wovoka described his vision: "When the sun died, I went up to heaven and saw God and all the people who had died a long time ago. God told me to come back and tell my people they must be good and love one an-

Burial of the dead after the Wounded Knee Massacre. The bodies were dumped unceremoniously in a common grave. Later, the descendants of those slain erected a monument which stands today. Photo by G.E. Trager.
(Courtesy Nebraska State Historical Society)

other, and not fight, or steal, or lie. He gave me this
dance to give to my people."

The dance Wovoka mentioned was later to be called
the Ghost dance, and his philosophy was spread rapidly
across the Plains. The new doctrine preached many
of the Christian morals and for good reason. Upon his
father's death, Wovoka, at the age of fourteen, had gone
to live with a white, Christian family named Wilson.
He had, in fact, adopted the name Jack Wilson. Not
only was he familiar with the beliefs of his people, the
Paiute; he soon became fluent in the teachings of Christ
through his adopted father's practice of reading the
Bible aloud to the family.

James Mooney, an ethnologist in the employ of the
Bureau of American Ethnology, met Wovoka during
his study of the Ghost dance in 1890–1891. His report
of the religion and the Sioux outbreak of 1890 was
first published as the Bureau's Fourteenth Annual Report. About Wovoka, he writes:

As he approached I saw that he was a young man,
a dark full-blood, compactly built, and taller than the
Paiute generally, being nearly 6 feet in height. He
was well dressed in white man's clothes, with the
broad-brimmed white felt hat common in the west,
secured on his head by means of a beaded ribbon
under the chin. . . He wore a good pair of boots. His
hair was cut off square on a line below the base
of the ears, after the manner of his tribe. His coun-
tenance was open and expressive of firmness and decision, but with no marked intellectuality. The
features were broad and heavy, very different from
the thin, clearcut features of the prairie tribes.

Chief Big Foot. In the below zero weather, the bodies quickly froze in horrid positions on the Wounded Knee Battlefield. Photo by G. E. Trager.

. . . He said he was about 35 years of age, fixing the date from a noted battle between the Paiute and the whites near Pyramid Lake, in 1860, at which time he said he was about the size of his little boy, who appeared to be of about 4 years. His father Tavibo, "White Man," was not a preacher, but was a *capita* [from the Spanish *capitan*] or petty chief, and was a dreamer and invulnerable. His own proper name from boyhood was Wovoka or Wüvoka, "The Cutter," but a few years ago he had assumed the name of his paternal grandfather, Kwohitsauq, or "Big Rumbling Belly."

When about 20 years of age, he married, and continued to work for Mr. Wilson. He had given the

[Ghost] dance to his people about four years before, but had received his great revelation about two years previously. On this occasion "the sun died" [was eclipsed] and he fell asleep in the daytime and was taken up to the other world. Here he saw God, with all the people who had died long ago engaged in their old-time sports and occupations, all happy and forever young. It was a pleasant land and full of game. After showing him all, God told him he must go back and tell his people they must be good and love one another, have no quarreling, and live in peace with the whites; that they must work, and not lie or steal; that they must put away all the old practices that savored of war; that if they faithfully obeyed his instructions they would at last be reunited with their friends in this other world, where there would be no more death or sickness or old age. He was then given the dance which he was commanded to bring back to his people.

The first Ghost dance was held on the Walker Lake Reservation in January, 1889. The people danced around in a circle, clasping hands. They soon fell into hypnotic trances and dreamed that they saw their ancestors. When they awoke, they composed songs about their visions of life in the other world.

The Ghost dance soon began to spread through other tribes living in Nevada and Oregon, and then east onto the Northern Plains. The Arapaho appear to be the first Plains tribe to hear about the dance, and delegates were sent to meet with Wovoka and learn more about the "new messiah" who was to come down to earth. Wovoka gave the delegates instructions about performing the

Sweat lodge framework and sacred pole used in the Ghost Dance. This photo was taken by James Mooney in 1892 at the Pine Ridge Reservation two years after the Wounded Knee Massacre.

dance and the essence of the Ghost dance doctrine. His message was written down by one Arapaho (free rendering by Mooney):

When you get home you must make a dance to continue five days. Dance four successive nights, and the last night keep up the dance until the morning of the fifth day, when all must bathe in the river and then disperse to their homes. You must all do in the same way.

I, Jack Wilson, love you all, and my heart is full of

gladness for the gifts you have brought me. . . . I give you a good spirit and give you all good paint. I want you to come again in three months, some from each tribe there [the Indian Territory].

Grandfather [a universal title of reverence among Indians and here meaning the messiah] says, when your friends die you must not cry. You must not hurt anybody or do harm to anyone. You must not fight. Do right always. It will give you satisfaction in life . . .

Do not tell the white people about this. Jesus is now upon the earth. He appears like a cloud. The dead are all alive again. I do not know when they will be here; maybe this fall or in the spring. When the time comes there will be no more sickness and everyone will be young again.

Do not refuse to work for the whites and do not make any trouble with them until you leave them. When the earth shakes [at the coming of the new world] do not be afraid. It will not hurt you.

I want you to dance every six weeks. Make a feast at the dance and have food that everybody may eat. Then bathe in the water. That is all. You will receive good words again from me sometime. Do not tell lies.

And so Wovoka's word reached the Northern Plains. The new doctrine was not accepted by the Blackfeet, Sarsi, Plains Ojibwa, Plains Cree, Crow and Eastern division of the Sioux. However, it was quickly embraced by the Assiniboine, Gros Ventre, Arikara, Hidatsa, Mandan, Cheyenne, Arapaho, and Western Sioux. Each tribe sent delegates to Wovoka to find out more about the coming of the new messiah. Hundreds of devotees met with the Paiute and listened to him preach. Although Wovoka spoke only his native dialect and broken English, the delegates claimed that when he spoke, each man could understand him in his own tribal tongue. As the word spread, many tribes believed that Wovoka, himself, was indeed, the reincarnation of Christ. Just as Wovoka had directed, the people returned to their reservations to spread the gospel of new hope for the Indian people.

Although the Indians of Nevada performed the dance precisely as it was taught by Wovoka, the neighboring tribes to the east began to add to the ceremony much of their indivdual tribal ritual. Those responsible for spreading the doctrine over the Northern Plains were Sage of the Arapaho, the Cheyenne Porcupine, and Short Bull and Kicking Bear of the Western Sioux. As a prelude to the Ghost dance proper, the Arapaho and Cheyenne performed the Crow dance, similar to the Grass dance, because someone had received a vision in which he saw crows dancing. The Sioux characteristically participated in the Sweat Lodge ceremony before doing the Ghost dance. Most tribes planted a sacred tree in the center of the dance area and adorned it with religious articles.

The most significant part of the Ghost dance was the hypnotic trance into which many of the dancers fell. While they were in the trance, they dreamed they visited with deceased relatives and awoke to compose songs about their mystical experiences. Here are some of the typical songs described by Mooney:

From the Arapaho:

My children, my children
Look! The earth is about to move
Look! The earth is about to move
My father tells me so
My father tells me so

Many of the dancers related events reminiscent of the old days such as hunting buffalo, or playing traditional games.

From the Cheyenne:

My comrade
My comrade
Let us go and play shinny
Let us go and play shinny
Let us look for our mother
Let us look for our mother
Our father tells us to do it
Our father tells us to do it

Another Cheyenne song preaches a stronger Christian concept:

The devil
The devil
We have put him aside
We have put him aside
The White Man above
The White Man above
He is our father
He is our father
He has blest us
He has blest us

Among the Sioux, dancers wore a particular garment

called the Ghost shirt made of buckskin or, more often, a flour sack. It was decorated with eagle feathers and designs symbolizing the crow, moon, and stars. It was believed that no bullet could penetrate the shirt. Many of the dancers also wore the plume of an eagle in their hair, believing that when the "earth turned over," the white men would be swallowed up by it, while those who wore the plume would go unharmed. Despite Wovoka's original doctrine of peace, it appears that, at least among the Sioux, the Indians were expecting some kind of violence to accompany the rebirth of the world.

Violence was soon to come. While most of the dances went on without incident, many of the government agents believed that the Indians were preparing for an uprising. The strange hypnotic trances and the dogma that the whites were to be consumed in some terrible upheaval only confirmed these suspicions. The white men living on reservations became uneasy.

One of the Indians who endorsed the Ghost dance movement was Sitting Bull. He had been living peacefully with the white man since his surrender in 1881. He had even traveled for a year with Buffalo Bill's Wild West Show as a feature attraction. But now he was living at Standing Rock, finding himself in a feud with the agent, James McLaughlin. McLaughlin was jealous and suspicious of Sitting Bull and would have welcomed any good reason for having the old chief imprisoned. The Ghost dance provided such a reason.

Sitting Bull was invited to Pine Ridge to meet the new messiah. He, according to the ruling then on reservations, requested a pass from the agent to leave Standing Rock. McLaughlin jumped at the chance to prove that Sitting Bull was involved in an uprising and immediately ordered the old chief arrested. On the morning of December 15, 1890, before dawn, Lieutenant Bull Head, in charge of a detachment of Indian police, arrived at Sitting Bull's cabin. Awakening the chief from a sound sleep, the police informed him that he was to be arrested. But Sitting Bull resisted the idea. "I will not go!" he cried out, alerting his followers in nearby houses. An onslaught immediately followed, and Sitting Bull, his seventeen-year-old son, Crowfoot, and 6 others were killed by police bullets. Like Crazy Horse before him, Sitting Bull met the treachery of the white man.

The death of Sitting Bull put fear into the hearts of all the Sioux. His followers joined the small band of Big Foot, another chief who might have remained obscure in the annals of Sioux history had it not been for the Ghost dance. Big Foot had been determined to go to Pine Ridge for a massive Ghost dance, but orders were issued to arrest him. En route to Pine Ridge he was intercepted at Wounded Knee Creek by Colonel J. W. Forsyth and, ironically, remnants of Custer's old Seventh Cavalry.

The chief, suffering from pneumonia, surrendered along with 106 warriors and 250 women and children. On the next day, December 29, 1890, Big Foot and his followers were surrounded by nearly 500 soldiers and four Hotchkiss guns, which had been strategically placed on a knoll overlooking the camp. The Indians were disarmed, routed of their tipis, and forced to stand out in the below-zero weather while the soldiers tore apart their bedding looking for concealed weapons. It was still early in the morning.

An old medicine man, frustrated at the indignity of

the circumstances, called out for the people to resist, reminding them that many wore Ghost Shirts, which would repel the soldiers' bullets. Quickly some soldiers attempted to quiet the old man, and in the melee, a shot was fired. Sudden panic ensued. A command was given, and the Hotchkiss guns exploded their shells in rapid tempo at the huddled group of women and children.

Frantically the Indians, even women and children, attempted to save their lives, fighting against the soldiers with clubs or anything else that would serve as a weapon. In desperation, many of them fled along the frozen creek bed. Some managed to escape, but before nine o'clock in the morning 40 men and 200 women and children had been slaughtered. The massacred remains of women and children were found as far as three miles from the camp, where they had been hounded by the soldiers and killed without mercy. The calm of death that prevailed at Wounded Knee was soon interrupted by a blizzard. When the weather cleared, the frozen bodies of the slain were collected in wagons and unceremoniously dumped in a common grave. As one officer remarked after the battle, "Now we have avenged Custer's death."

Although Colonel Forsyth was charged with misconduct for permitting the murder of defenseless women and children, he was ultimately exonerated. In addition, 23 soldiers were awarded the Congressional Medal of Honor for "heroic action" at Wounded Knee.

A few skirmishes followed the tragedy, but for the most part of the Indian wars of the West were ended on this black day.

Today, one may visit two monuments which stand on the bleak Plains. One has been erected to Custer

and the valiant Seventh who met their defeat against
the Sioux and Cheyenne at the Little Big Horn. Each
summer the Crow reenact the "massacre" for the benefit of visiting tourists. The United States Government,
as part of its Mission 66 program, has restored much of
the battlefield and has built a museum and tourist
facility for visitors. A marked trail takes the guest along
the route that Custer and his men journeyed that fateful
day. White tombstones mark the places where the soldiers of the Seventh are buried. Descriptive markers tell
about each detail of the battle.

Three hundred miles to the southeast, another memo-
rial stands which bears the inscription: THIS MONU-
MENT IS ERECTED BY SURVIVING RELATIVES AND OTHER
OGLALA AND CHEYENNE RIVER SIOUX INDIANS IN
MEMORIAL OF THE CHIEF BIG FOOT MASSACRE,
DECEMBER 29, 1890.

A cement curb has been built around the common
grave, and on Memorial Day, descendants of the massacred Indians bring flowers and strew them on the
crude final resting place. On the peaceful knoll where
the Hotchkiss guns rained their terror down on the
helpless people, a Catholic church now stands, casting
its silent shadow over the spirits of Big Foot and his
band.

12 The White Man's Road

IN 1824, during President Andrew Jackson's administration, the Bureau of Indian Affairs, sometimes called the Indian Service, was organized. Because of recurring hostility between Indians and whites, the agency was logically established as part of the War Department. Later, with the inauguration of the Department of Interior in 1849, the Bureau came under jurisdiction of the Secretary of Interior.

In 1880 Indian land totaled approximately 241,000,-000 acres, an area nearly the size of Indiana. The Bureau's program emphasized "civilizing" the American Indians by teaching them how to farm. The Bureau, acting as an arm of the "Great White Father" in Washington, D.C., served its "Indian children" in a paternalistic fashion which is still evident today. Dedicated to "assimilating the American Indian into the mainstream of American society," Congress passed the General Allotment Act of 1887. It provided that reservation land be divided among individual Indian owners. This act made it possible for Indians to sell their land to the highest bidder.

The results were catastrophic. Between 1887 and

1934, the Indians lost nearly 190,000,000 acres, four-fifths of all their land, to white men. Twenty-seven million acres alone were appropriated by the Federal Government for use as national parks. By the time the Indian Reorganization Act was passed in 1934, the Indians owned slightly more than 50,000,000 acres of land, an area approximately equal to New Jersey and the New England states combined.

In 1964 there were nearly 300 separate areas of land reserved for Indian use, ranging from small colonies comprising only a few acres, to the larger reservations, some of which total more than 1,000,000 acres each. Most of the Northern Plains Indians live on approximately 20 reservations in the states of Montana, North Dakota, South Dakota, Wyoming, and the prairie provinces of Canada. The largest reservation is Pine Ridge with nearly 1,500,000 acres. It ranks in size second only to the Navajo Reservation.

Current estimates (1967) approximate the total Indian population in the United States at 700,000, a decided increase since the turn of the century when they numbered about 200,000. Many authorities predict, at the current rate of population increase, that there will be more Indians by the year 2000 than in pre-Columbian times. The Bureau of Indian Affairs distinguishes between Indians who actually reside on the reservations and those who are enrolled in tribes but live and work in off-reservation communities. According to the bureau's statistics, about 400,000 Indians live on reservations (380,000 in 1964). The combined number of Northern Plains Indians living in the 4 reservation states (including enrolled tribal members, as well as residents) is about 100,000.

Each reservation, for the most part, is governed by a

tribal council made up of Indian representatives elected by Indian people living in their respective districts. The Bureau of Indian Affairs still maintains branch offices on the reservations under the supervision of a superintendent. In most cases, the superintendents are white men, but in recent years Indians have been named to these positions. While the Indians are not technically wards of the United States, their land is held in trust by the Federal Government. While in theory, being citizens of the United States, Indians are allowed to leave and return to the reservation at will and conduct their own business affairs, in practice, all business transactions conducted on the reservations must receive the approval of the local superintendent. Many Indians feel that this is an injustice, claiming that many of the representatives of the Bureau are uninterested in Indian affairs and that often the fate of the individual Indian is at the mercy of an unconcerned white man.

On the other hand, the Indians fight desperately at recurring proposals by Congressmen to terminate Indian reservations. The Indians prefer to gamble on treatment by the Federal Government, rather than face the possibility of their affairs being administered by individual states. Currently, 13 states have jurisdiction over Indians living within their borders, but none on the Northern Plains. On Federally administered reservations, even Federal jurisdiction is limited. Most reservations have their own tribal courts, judges, and police to attend to minor offenses, while Federal jurisdiction applies only to serious crimes, such as murder. With approval of the Secretary of the Interior, tribes are permitted to hire attorneys-at-law to represent them in claims against the United States Government. In 1946

Congress established the Indian Claims Commission, an agency independent of the Bureau of Indian Affairs, to evaluate claims by tribes against the United States and make payments to tribes for lands appropriated by the white man. The commission is still actively reviewing Indian claims and has made a number of payments to tribes and bands based on the value of the land at the time the treaty was negotiated.

Living conditions on any of the reservations is often likely to shock a casual visitor. The majority of Indians live in substandard housing, have the lowest income of any ethnic group, and a life-span of only forty-four years of age. There is a particularly high rate of alcoholism, tuberculosis, and venereal disease. Good sanitation practices are almost unheard of, with a minimum of electrical and indoor plumbing facilities available. In this day and age of prosperity, one may justifiably ask why.

The reasons for poverty on Indian reservations are a combination of many problems, mostly social and psychological. Even in the twentieth century the average Indian lives a dual role; he is exposed, on the one hand, to the wonders of the white man's technology, yet he is bound by tradition and environment to what he most often refers to as the Indian way. Each day the reservation Indian is faced with a conflict in culture. Part of the time, through education and indoctrination, he acts out the role of the white man. He wears the white man's clothing and, if he is lucky, works at a white man's job. Yet when he returns to his own home, his social surroundings often change drastically. He speaks his native language, participates in the customs of his tribe, and measures his progress in life by Indian values. Despite the teaching of the white man, the propaganda of the Bureau of Indian Affairs, and the precognition that he is destined to become acculturated and join the mainstream of American society, he prefers to assert his Indianness. In short, he has walked the white man's road for more than 100 years, only to find at the end of his journey that he is still inconvertibly an Indian.

The Indian has an ethnic pride unparalleled in all the world. With very few exceptions, the Indian refuses to demonstrate on behalf of his civil rights. Indian leaders have made it clear that their people do not particularly want to integrate. The government has set up a program encouraging Indians to relocate in urban areas, where they may receive vocational training and, eventually, good jobs. While many Indians are lured to the cities in hopes of attaining employment and leaving the drudgery and boredom of reservation life, the majority return to the reservations. They soon become disenchanted with the white man's world, the city slums, the fact that they are often unidentifiable as American Indians, and most of all, the fact that they are strangers in a strange world. Some of the Northern Plains Indians migrate to such cities as Chicago, Denver, and Los Angeles and stay, but for most the pattern is inevitable. They live in miniscule "Indian towns," where there is a high degree of alcoholism, poverty, and hopelessness. They long for their relatives and friends back home and the opportunity to simply see their own land, speak their own language. Soon, without the slightest provocation, they leave the big city for the reservation life.

Employment on the reservations is scarce. Some

Indians work for the bureau in the local offices; others hire out to white ranchers and farmers nearby during the planting and harvest seasons. Most Indians receive incomes from land they lease to white farmers and ranchers. Indian customs still prevail, and the man who is lucky enough to hold a good job, for which he receives a salary comparable to a white man, often must share his earnings with relatives who are less fortunate. Kinship systems are generally more encompassing than in the white world, and the breadwinner often shares his food and money with a distant cousin and other remote relations not usually recognized in the white man's society.

In recent years the Federal Government has promoted the establishment of light industry on Indian reservations to combat the shortage of employment. This is essentially the only way that the Indian may stay on the reservation and still be able to obtain a good job. Several industries are already underway on the Northern Plains reservations. The Bulova Watch Company operates a plant on the Turtle Mountain Reservation in North Dakota. The Five Star Cheese Corporation employs Standing Rock Sioux to produce cheddar cheese and milk products. U.S. Automatics, Inc., has an electronics plant on the Crow Indian Reservation in Montana. The Guild Arts and Crafts Company at Ashland, Montana, employs Cheyenne Indians to make plastic products. Wright and McGill, manufacturers of fishhooks, have three factories on the Pine Ridge Sioux Reservation in South Dakota.

But this is only a beginning; there are still many occupational snags to overcome. Many white employers, for instance, find Indian employees "unreliable." This is mainly a result of 100 years of conditioning. Along with the continuing paternalism by the Bureau of Indian Affairs, most Indian youngsters have never been raised in a household where they see their father leave every morning for work and return later with a paycheck. The concept of nine to five is still hazy. The Indian also inadvertently adheres to the concept called Indian time. While often treated lightly by Indians themselves, Indian time is very real. It usually signifies a nonspecific time of day. If a dance, for instance, began at seven o'clock in the evening, Indian time, you can very well arrive at nine o'clock and not be late. Tardiness is unknown in Indian society, because being on time is insignificant. For all practical purposes, "ontimemanship" is a white man's concept. One can easily tell the Indian progressives from the conservatives by their promptness.

More than one industry has experienced the frustration of combatting Indian time. The results have usually been detrimental to the tribes on whose land the industry is located. One factory, owned by a white man, decided to open a branch on an Indian reservation. At first, prospects looked good. He had no trouble hiring eager Indian employees. A few months went by, and there was a sharp increase in tardiness and absenteeism. In order to meet production schedules, the manufacturer had to resort to hiring white employees from nearby towns. Even though the factory was located on the reservation, it brought in no revenue to the tribe other than the lease money.

The United States Public Housing Administration, in cooperation with tribally operated housing authorities, has made some strides in providing adequate homes for Indian people on reservations. Prefabricated houses, which include indoor plumbing facilities, multiple bedrooms, and electricity, are slowly replacing the traditional one-room log cabins and frame houses with sod roofs and floors. But the job is far from completion.

Housing developments similar to those found in average white, middle-class communities are beginning to appear on the reservations. But many of the older people prefer to live in their traditional homes. Many still sleep in four-wall tents and tipis in the summertime, which serve to augment their small houses. By far, the majority of Indians still live in cramped quarters, sleeping five to ten to a room. Sanitation is a continuing problem, even in the newer developments. Despite the attempts of individual tribes to give leadership to cleanup campaigns, most of the homes on reservations are beyond repair. Improper garbage disposal and decaying outhouses cultivate additional health hazards.

The United States Public Health Service maintains hospitals and mobile medical units, as well as competent staffs of doctors, technicians, and nurses for all Indian people. Indigent Indians are not required to pay for medical services, yet many diseases which are no longer a threat to the average white community run rampant on the reservations. Much of this is due to negligence on the part of the Indians and the absence of clear communications between them and the non-Indian medical practitioners.

The older Indians' traditional notion about the white man is one of awe. Nurtured by the prevailing paternalistic attitudes of the Bureau of Indians Affairs, the Indians sometimes believe that the almighty white man is gifted with something akin to magical powers. This is especially true of their beliefs about white doctors. Generally, the Indian feels that the white medical man is, or should be, capable of diagnosing a patient's symptoms immediately and treating him successfully in a very short time.

Consequently, when an Indian patient is brought into a public health hospital with some unknown disease, an attempt by the physician to take time to run tests and observe the patient often results in suspicion and frustration. He expects the doctor immediately to make a diagnosis, prescribe the proper medicine, and dismiss him. If the doctor cannot comply with the Indian's demand for expediency, the patient often angrily leaves the hospital against medical advice and consults one of the local medicine men, or shamans, who will at least give him psychological relief from whatever ails him.

Often, too, an Indian who is relieved of the symptoms of a disorder feels cured and will refuse to continue taking a medication prescribed by the doctor. Many die of diseases such as diabetes, because they see no immediate need to take insulin once they are on the road to recovery.

The important role the local medicine man plays in the lives of Indian people today cannot be ignored. In many cases, some of the older people refuse even to consult a white doctor, because they rely on the skill of the medicine man to relieve their symptoms. Since even white doctors agree that fifty percent of most office cases suffer from psychosomatic disorders, the medicine men probably do as good a job as any of their white counterparts—in half their cases. However, many Indians die from organic diseases because of their refusal to trust the white doctors.

Just as the medicine man seemingly works against the health authorities, he can also work for them. A patient seeking aid from a native practitioner is often advised by the medicine man to go to the hospital for treatment. If the patient agrees and he is cured by the white doctor, the medicine man can still take credit for curing him. After all, it was *his* decision for the patient to see a white doctor. I know of several occasions where Sioux shamans accompanied their patients to the local hospital to assist in the diagnosis of their patients' disorders.

Obviously, many of the Indian problems on reservations can be solved through education. It is no wonder then that the Bureau of Indian Affairs spends more than half its budget on educating Indian children. In addition to Federal schools on the reservations, Indian children also attend mission and public schools. The conditions are similar to those being faced in non-Indian communities across the nation: overcrowded classrooms, shortage of teachers, and the inevitable dropout. The rate of dropout is extremely high on reservations where initiative and incentive to go on to jobs after graduation are dismally low. Many start school at an older age than their white counterparts, and a great number of them have difficulty with the English language. Nevertheless, more and more are completing grammar and high school and are going on to institutions of higher learning.

To further combat the problems of disease, poverty, unemployment, and inadequate education, President Lyndon Johnson specifically named the American Indian as one of the groups to receive assistance in his War on Poverty program. The Office of Economic Opportunity has made available to the Indian people most of its programs, including VISTA Volunteers, Neighborhood Youth Corps, Conservation Corps, and Community Action Programs, all of which are administered by Indians themselves. As a result of these programs, many new jobs have opened up on the reservations, but not without difficulty. Many of the older conservatives argue that all the good jobs go to mixed bloods, that "if you have an Indian name (such as Big Crow, Blue Horse), you won't be hired." There is possibly some truth in this, inasmuch as the mixed bloods, descendants of the early traders who took Indian wives, share a white man's point of view more readily than a conservative full blood. Others argue, that the youth programs are corrupting their children. A boy enrolled in the Neighborhood Youth Corps, for example, may very well earn more money than his father. Since parental influence is waning, many children are even less controllable, because they have money to spend. Some youngsters, knowing that according to Indian custom, they will have to share their salary with other relatives, often spend their entire paycheck as soon as they receive it. Often, it is squandered in some off-reservation bar.

Alcoholism has often been called the number one Indian problem. The myth that Indians are biologically inferior to the white man when it comes to holding one's liquor has been perpetuated for more than a century. This, of course, is a fallacy. What causes Indians to drink are the same things that motivate peoples of other ethnic backgrounds: depression, a feeling of futility, oppression, loneliness, and boredom. Because Indians are somewhat isolated on reservations, these emotional disturbances are not only magnified, but contagious. Social drinking, for instance, is largely unknown by Indians. Ever since the Indian traders carrying their supply of cheap liquor invaded the Northern Plains, the Indian has consumed "fire water" only to get drunk. So ominous was the threat of "drunken Indians" that the sale of liquor was prohibited to Indians by Federal law until Congress repealed it in 1953. This, of course, encouraged bootlegging at exhorbitant prices. After the law was repealed, tribes were given the option of legalizing the sale of liquor, but most chose not to permit it on reservation land. However, Indians may simply cross the line to the nearest off-reservation town and buy as much as they like. Bootlegging is still practiced on many of the reservations by unscrupulous Indians and white men.

Alcoholism, although a serious problem in itself, leads to even greater social disasters. High rates of crime, juvenile delinquency, sexual promiscuity, and broken homes are common on all reservations, most of them a direct result of drinking. I have always been amazed in my frequent trips to the reservations to discover that after an Indian celebration on Saturday night, possibly 100 to 200 Indians are thrown in jail because of drunkenness. On one reservation, the Indian police station themselves on the main highway that leads from the agency to the nearest "white" town and wait for drunks to leave the bars. In addition to arresting the offenders, they more often than not have to conduct the small children who accompanied their intoxicated parents back to the reservation. There is often a great deal of levity in talking about drinking because it is so common. Young boys, pressured by the taunts of their friends, often simply get drunk and thrown in jail as part of their attempts to prove they are mature.

In spite of the seeming depression on Indian reservations, the Indian people are able to enjoy life. The Northern Plains tribes have been active recently in a rejuvenation of Indian culture. Sun dances and smaller powwows and Indian fairs are the highlights of the summertime activities. The piercing of the Sun dance was reinstated in 1959 among the Oglala Sioux and Turtle Mountain Plains Ojibwa, without objection by the government. Indian religions are still popular despite the teaching of missionaries. Living in the revolving door of two cultures makes it relatively simple for most Indians to believe in more than one form of worship. Many of the same Indians who partake in the Sun dance, Sweat Lodge, and vision quest, show up in church on Sunday morning. One quasi-Christian assembly called the Native American Church is popular to some degree on Northern Plains reservations. Although it does not exert the influence on the Northern Plains as it does in the south, the Native American Church has many followers. The ceremonies are usually conducted in a tipi; Indian songs are sung, and the members pray to Jesus Christ. An important part of the ritual is the taking of the "Eucharist," which is the hallucinogenic drug, peyote, imported from the Southern Plains and Mexico. By eating the "buttons" of this plant, the members receive technicolor visions in their communion with God. The terminology and doctrine is largely Christian; however, the religious paraphernalia, including water drums, gourd rattles, and feather fans, are native Indian. The Native American Church has a

Federal charter, and Indians in most states are permitted to use the drug, because it is part of their religious beliefs. Indians partaking of the drug consider it strictly a form of religious communion and are shocked to discover that there are white people who take the drug indiscreetly.

The Native American Church is usually considered a part of an overall movement called Pan-Indianism, which is essentially an indirect attempt to unite all Indian tribes into a singlar nationalistic entity. The movement, if it is rightly termed, most often takes the form of an Indian cultural exchange. Similarities in music, dance, and costumes are noticeable at many of the larger Indian celebrations. But there are greater political and economic implications. Some Indians believe that the tribes must unite to lobby for common goals. Organizations, such as the National Congress of American Indians and the National Indian Youth Council, have large memberships representing most tribes. They meet regularly to discuss forthcoming Indian legislation and the problems common to their reservations. Another organization run by non-Indians, the Association on American Indian Affairs, is also active in defending Indian civil rights and indignities. One of its many diverse programs includes making newspaper and magazine editors aware that many cartoons of Indians in their publications are offensive to the Indian people. They were particularly instrumental in stopping an advertising campaign which featured an Indian selling a smooth "fire water." In view of the alcohol problem among Indians, the association's demand was quickly met and the campaign shelved at great cost to the manufacturer and advertising agency.

The Bureau of Indian Affairs has been particularly active in promoting tourism on Indian reservations. The Indians' renewed interest in their own songs, dances, and arts and crafts has become an inducement for white tourists to visit reservations. The Northern Plains tribes are especially active sponsors of celebrations. The Blackfeet host the North American Indian Days at Browning, Montana, in July. The Crow hold their annual Sun dance at Lodge Grass, Montana, in June, and the Crow Indian Fair and Rodeo at Crow Agency, Montana, in August. The Cree have their Sun dance at Box Elder, Montana, in June, and the Cheyenne Sun dance is held at Lame Deer, Montana, in July. The Plains Ojibwa hold their Sun dance at Belcourt, North Dakota in June, and the Oglala Sioux Sun dance is held at Pine Ridge, South Dakota, in August.

There are usually powwows held in conjunction with all major national holidays. Indian Grass dances traditionally follow the Sun dances. The All-American Indian Days, held at Sheridan, Wyoming, in August, attracts many of the Northern Plains tribes where they perform traditional tribal dances and play Indian games. Each year, judges select Miss Indian America from a host of tribal contestants.

In addition to the Indian ceremonies, many of the reservations own attractive camping grounds with a number of outdoor sports facilities. Many of them are near historic landmarks and national parks and monuments. There is a camping area on the Crow Indian Reservation, Crow Agency, Montana, near the Custer Battlefield National Monument, and Fort C. F. Smith, which was one of the forts established to protect the Bozeman Trail during the Red Cloud War. On the

Pine Ridge Reservation in South Dakota, visitors may follow the Big Foot Trail, which leads to the Wounded Knee Battlefield and Museum. On the neighboring Rosebud Reservation there are a number of facilities for hiking, swimming, fishing, and horseback riding. The Blackfeet Reservation has a number of recreational facilities, including the Museum of the Plains Indian at Browning, Montana. The reservation is bordered by Glacier National Park.

Visiting an Indian reservation can be very rewarding. The people are fine hosts and never seem to be too busy to tell visitors about their tribal heritage. Entering their homes is like discovering new worlds. There, amidst the anachronisms of modern conveniences, is a drum, war-bonnet, or large picture frame crammed with photographs of heroes now gone—the grandfather who was chief of his band; an uncle who served as a scout for the United States. Next to the frame is a plaque bearing the white man entreaty, GOD BLESS OUR HOME. In one room the children watch their fate on a television Western. In another, an old man puffs on a long-stemmed pipe and tells it the way it really happened. Constant reminders of both red and white cultures are found everywhere: automobiles and horses, frame houses and tipis, churches and sweat lodges, doctors and medicine men. Positive that he is not a white man, but insecure with his Indianness, the red man follows the white man's road in constant search of the Indian way.

Acknowledgments

The author wishes to thank the following persons for their valuable assistance in preparing this book:

Richard H. Shryock, chairman of the Phillips subcommittee, American Philosophical Society, whose association graciously supported my field work at Pine Ridge and Rosebud, South Dakota, during the summers of 1966 and 1967;

William C. Sturtevant, Smithsonian Institution; Dell Hymes, University of Pennsylvania; and Gertrude P. Kurath, Dance Research Center, Ann Arbor, for their endorsement of my Sioux project, the results of which are partially reported in this book;

George Plenty Wolf, William Horn Cloud, and Oliver Red Cloud, Oglala Sioux from Pine Ridge, South Dakota; and Sidney Willow and Joe Shakes Spear, Arapho from Wind River, Wyoming, who provided information on contemporary music, dance, and religion;

Margaret C. Blaker, archivist, Smithsonian Institution, and her staff, for their help in obtaining old photographs and manuscripts;

Roni Godwin, for her editorial assistance and preparation of the manuscript;

My wife, Marla, for devoted assistance in field research and her constant inspiration.

W.K.P.

248

Bibliography

Bass, Althea, *The Arapaho Way*. New York, Clarkson N. Potter, Inc., 1966.

Catlin, George, *Letters and Notes on the North American Indians*. Minneapolis, Ross and Haines, Inc., 1965.

Denig, Edwin T., *Five Indian Tribes of the Upper Missouri*. Norman, University of Oklahoma Press, 1961.

Dorsey, G. A., "The Arapaho Sun Dance." *Fieldiana: Anthropology,* Vol. IV (1903), 1-228.

Ewers, John C., *Artists of the Old West*. New York, Doubleday and Company, Inc., 1965.

———, "Blackfeet Crafts." Washington, D.C., United States Government Printing Office, 1945.

———, *The Blackfeet: Raiders of the Northwestern Plains*. Norman, University of Oklahoma Press, 1958.

———, "The Horse in Blackfoot Culture." Washington, D.C., Bureau of American Ethnology, Bulletin 159.

———, "The Story of the Blackfeet." Washington, D.C., United States Government Printing Office, 1944.

Graham, Colonel W. A., *The Custer Myth*. Harrisburg, Stackpole Company, 1954.

Grinnell, George B., *Blackfoot Lodge Tales*. Lincoln, University of Nebraska Press, 1962.

———, *By Cheyenne Campfires*. New Haven, Yale University Press, 1962.

———, *The Cheyenne Indians*. 2 vols. New York, Cooper Square Publishers, 1965.

———, *The Fighting Cheyennes*. Norman, University of Oklahoma Press, 1956.

249

HOEBEL, E. ADAMSON, *The Cheyennes: Indians of the Great Plains*. New York, Holt, Rinehart and Winston, Inc., 1960.

HYDE, GEORGE E., *A Sioux Chronicle*. Norman, University of Oklahoma Press, 1956.

———, *Red Cloud's Folk*. Norman, University of Oklahoma Press, 1957.

———, *Indians of the High Plains*. Norman, University of Oklahoma Press, 1959.

———, *Spotted Tail's Folk*. Norman, University of Oklahoma Press, 1961.

KING, CHARLES, *Campaigning with Crook*. Norman, University of Oklahoma Press, 1964.

LABARRE, WESTON, *The Peyote Cult*. Hamden, Conn., The Shoe String Press, 1964.

LLEWELLYN, KARL N., and HOEBEL, E. ADAMSON, *The Cheyenne Way*. Norman, University of Oklahoma Press, 1961.

LONG, JAMES LARPENTEUR, *The Assiniboines*. Michael Steven Kennedy, ed. Norman, University of Oklahoma Press, 1961.

LOWIE, ROBERT H., *Indians of the Plains*. New York, Doubleday and Company, Inc., 1954.

———, *The Crow Indians*. New York, Holt, Rinehart and Winston, Inc., 1956.

LYFORD, CARRIE A., "Quill and Beadwork of the Western Sioux." Washington, D.C., United States Government Printing Office, 1940.

McNITT, FRANK, *The Indian Traders*. Norman, University of Oklahoma Press, 1963.

MOONEY, JAMES, *Ghost Dance Religion and the Sioux Outbreak of 1890*. Chicago, University of Chicago Press, 1965.

NEIHARDT, JOHN G., *Black Elk Speaks*. Lincoln, University of Nebraska Press, 1961.

OLSON, JAMES C., *Red Cloud and the Sioux Problem*. Lincoln, University of Nebraska Press, 1965.

ORCHARD, WILLIAM C., *Beads and Beadwork of the American Indian*. New York, Museum of the American Indian, Heye Foundation, 1929.

POWERS, WILLIAM K., *Indian Dancing and Costumes*. New York, G. P. Putnam's Sons, 1966.

ROE, FRANK GILBERT, *The Indian and the Horse*. Norman, University of Oklahoma Press, 1962.

SANDOZ, MARI, *Cheyenne Autumn*. New York, Hastings House, Publishers, Inc., 1953.

———, *Crazy Horse*. New York, Hastings House, Publishers, Inc., 1955.

———, *The Battle of the Little Big Horn*. Philadelphia, J. B. Lippincott Company, 1966.

SCHMITT, MARTIN F., and BROWN, DEE, *Fighting Indians of the West*. New York, Charles Scribner's Sons, 1955.

SPIER, LESLIE, *Plains Indian Parfleche Design*. Seattle, University of Washington Press, 1931.

STEWART, EDGAR I., *Custer's Luck*. Norman, University of Oklahoma Press, 1965.

UTLEY, ROBERT M., *The Last Days of the Sioux Nation*. New Haven, Yale University Press, 1963.

VESTAL, STANLEY, *Sitting Bull: Champion of the Sioux*. Norman, University of Oklahoma Press, 1965.

WELLMAN, PAUL, *Indian Wars of the West*. New York, Doubleday and Company, Inc., 1954.

WILDSCHUT, WILLIAM, and EWERS, JOHN C., *Crow Indian Beadwork*. New York, Museum of the American Indian, Heye Foundation, 1959.

WILL, GEORGE F., and HYDE, GEORGE E., *Corn Among the Indians of the Upper Missouri*. Lincoln, University of Nebraska Press, 1964.

Index

The Author

William K. Powers has spent sixteen years researching the lives of American Indians, living with them on their reservations and studying their histories. He has written numerous articles on various phases of Indian culture and is the author of a popular book published by Putnam's, *Here Is Your Hobby: Indian Dancing*. Mr. Powers is on the staff of *Boys' Life* magazine. With his wife and two young sons, he lives in Kendall Park, New Jersey.

Indians of the Northern Plains

The American Indian of the Northern Plains has impressed the world with his magnificent eagle feather warbonnet, his ability to ride bareback at breakneck speeds. In modern times he has had great influence on Indians in other parts of the country. Today, among most tribes, to be Indian is synonymous with being a Plains Indian. But it was not always so, author William K. Powers reveals in his history of the peoples of the Northern Plains. In this absorbing account, Powers, long a student of Indian culture discusses tribal life both today and in the past.

The *American Indian Life* Series is designed to introduce you to the principal American Indian tribes as they lived before and after the arrival of the white man.

White Horse, a Cheyenne Indian photographed by William Din-widdie of the Bureau of American Ethnology in 1895. Combining Indian and white clothing was typical of this period. Broad-brimmed hats were especially popular.